julia bradbury's

WAINWRIGHT WALKS

COAST TO COAST

I dedicate this book to all my lovely supporters and fellow walkers. Thank you for sharing your own adventures with me as well as your thoughts and ideas on the programmes. I must also acknowledge the many kind and caring people who sent gifts and good wishes when our son Zephyrus was born. Finally my particular thanks to the outdoor and walking enthusiasts who have helped, and are still helping my television walks to endure. You can plan and execute a long distance walk such as a Coast to Coast, but as with life, don't forget to expect the unexpected (and enjoy the view!).

Frances Lincoln Ltd
www.franceslincoln.com

A catalogue record for this book is available from the British Library.

ISBN: 978-0-7112-3380-5

Printed and bound in China

9 8 7 6 5 4 3 2 1

Right: The lighthouse at St Bees Head
Pages2-3: St Bees Bay from the Coast to Coast path on South Head

CONTENTS

Introduction 8

St Bees to Rosthwaite 18

Rosthwaite to Shap 40

Shap to Keld 62

Keld to Richmond 82

Richmond to Blakey Ridge 102

Blakey Ridge to Robin Hood's Bay 122

Index 142

Fleswick Bay

A
COAST TO COAST
WALK

INTRODUCTION

A long distance walk is a very different proposition to a one-dayer. The calculations vis-à-vis what to squeeze into your backpack are nul and void when you have to plan an almost three-week adventure across the country. How far can I walk each day? What sort of weight can I manage on my back over eight hour intervals? Where is the best pie and pint on the route? Will this be better than a fortnight somewhere sunny? All questions that only you can answer – but Alfred Wainwright has done a lot of the hard work for you.

Wainwright laboured long and hard to create a continuous walk linking England's east and west coasts, including three National Parks. He famously said that he finished the Pennine Way with relief, a Coast to Coast with regret. Eric Robson, film maker, writer, he of Radio 4's *Gardeners' Question Time* fame, walked the route in the 80s with the great Pipe Smoker himself for another television series – so he not only knows a bit about the physical trait of the challenge, he also enjoys an insight into Wainwright's preoccupation with this walk. Eric told me how fond and proud of a Coast to Coast AW was and how he certainly never completed this 'journey of delight' in the twelve days that he proposed was possible!

This LDW (long-distance walk) was Alfred Wainwright's retirement project. He stopped working as Kendal Borough Treasurer in 1967 having achieved prominence as a number cruncher for the council and an author. His seven *Pictorial Guides* to the Lake District are widely regarded as mini-masterpieces – all written and sketched over weekends and

Julia at St Bees

days off. In the early 70s he was ready for another project. Something to occupy the majority of his time now the bean counting was over. What a decade to create a LDW…The Beatles broke up, Microsoft was founded, President Nixon resigned in light of the Watergate scandal and Elvis was found dead on the loo. But above it all, a Coast to Coast was born. *A*, not *The* you'll note.

192 miles (308.9 kilometres) on foot is a test for any instep. To make it easier on yourself, follow Wainwright's suggestion and walk with the prevailing conditions in your favour departing from St Bees in the west and heading to Robin Hood's Bay in the east. He preferred to have the wind on his back rather than blowing in his face although he did lament the fact that perhaps 'the grandest part of it, through Lakeland comes so early'. I wouldn't worry, the heather moors of North Yorkshire ain't a bad place to finish. Don't feel compelled to follow AW's plan however, if you're going to do this – do it your way. He was always the first to encourage people to make their own plans, plot their own routes and follow their own noses.

It is tradition (if you do start from St Bees) to dip your toes in the sea and take a pebble with you for the duration to throw in the bay at the other end, although geologists are now urging people not to do that because of pebble disruption* (*completely made up term). I suppose you could take your own? If you can verify its provenance and vow to do a fake throw at the finish. I admit to taking one from St Bees and chucking it in the North Sea on camera, but I promise to return it one day. Of course it's not about the pebble – it's about the memories and experiences you end up with. I'm exceedingly lucky, my Coast to Coast was filmed so I have a

INTRODUCTION

Falling Foss

Cliffs near Robin Hood's Bay

permanent reminder of our endeavours, but of course there were oodles of moments that didn't get recorded. When we set off, a couple were embarking on their honeymoon from St Bees. A pretty blonde had a bunch of battered yellow flowers poking out of her backpack, her handsome husband held her hand protectively. Refreshingly they didn't want to appear on camera – they just wanted to get on with their first escapade as a married couple. (I often wonder what they said to each other as they passed Sellafield, one of the world's first nuclear power stations.) This scarred land that you encounter early on was once the home of iron and coal mines, now walking is the industry and thanks to AW tens of thousands of people pass through every year, although he probably wouldn't be happy about that. Back in the 70s he said that the Pennine Way was fast losing its original appeal as a wilderness walk and had become 'a too popular parade'.

When planning the walk Wainwright initially had four objectives:

1) to avoid towns
2) to link together three national parks
3) to keep to high ground wherever practical (or practicable as he writes it)
4) to use only rights of way and areas of open access

When I set out my four objectives were:
1) to avoid swearing on camera
2) to link together Wainwright's thoughts with my own less coherent notions
3) to maintain the moral high ground in order to wind up the crew wherever and whenever possible
4) to use only well hidden locations to pee
4b) to incite a new generation of hikers to embark on an adventure or get the oldies to do it again

Of all the television programmes I have made over the years there is no doubt that the walks have generated the biggest reaction of all. I completed my Coast to Coast four years ago and the series first transmitted in 2009. Since then it has been countless times and I am thrilled that people still react. I received the following email from a very proud grandmother:

Dear Ms Bradbury,
In 1986 my son Matthew, aged eleven and my husband David completed A Coast to Coast Walk in 'fine style' (Alfred Wainwright's words). I wrote to him as I was so proud of their

Imogen Austen – the next Julia Bradbury?

achievement and I received a delightful letter back from him congratulating them both.

David was determined to retrace his steps with our first-born grandchild Imogen. This August just after her eleventh birthday they both completed A Coast to Coast Walk in thirteen days. … The pair climbed Helvellyn via Striding Edge, managed to walk from Patterdale to Shap in one day and did 23 miles on one occasion. That day I will never forget. Having walked across the Vale of Mowbray, Imogen ran down the hill into Ingleby Cross, waving her walking pole and yelling 'Grandma!' Her stamina and determination was unstoppable.

It was a tremendous achievement for both of them, David is now 65 and has an artificial hip, so in the excitement of seeing our granddaughter walking all that way we tended to forget it was a great challenge for him too.

Imogen's ambition is to be a television presenter, maybe she will one day be the next Julia Bradbury?

Best wishes
Jennie Austen

And that dear reader is what it is all about. Creating memories of a lifetime. Completing a voyage with loved ones or friends, or flying solo as Wainwright prescribed. Do it your way; in modest segments, camp under the stars, go from pub to pub, however you do it, rely on your own resources and satisfy your own wisdoms and follies. It may be according to Wainwright, 'a walk in possession of feminine characteristics', but this is a man-sized adventure – and it's yours for the taking. Felicitations walkers (men, women and young 'uns)… best boot forward.

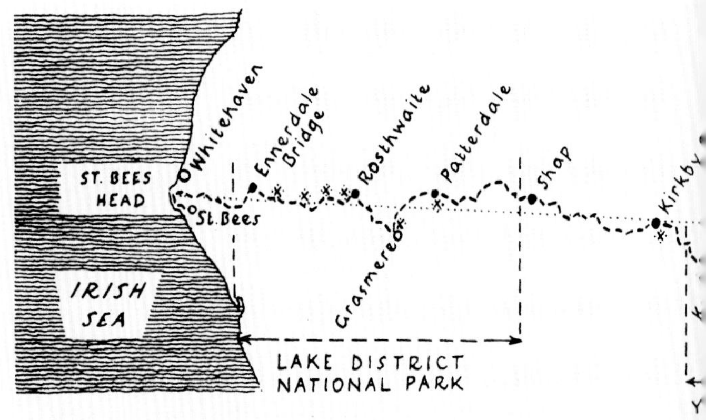

ALTITUDES

(Vertical scale greatly exaggerated)

The highest point reached is Kidsty Pike, 2560'

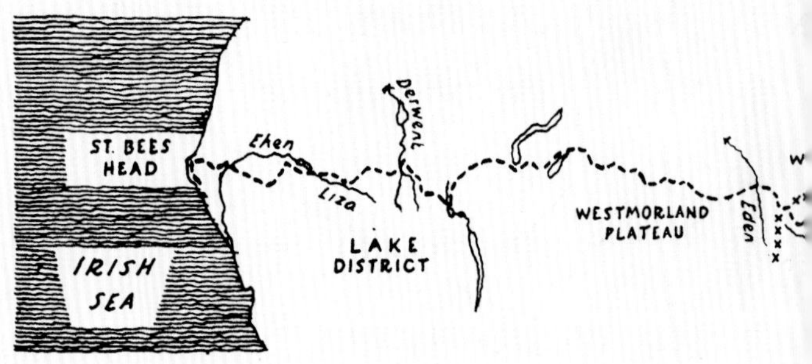

THE ROUTE

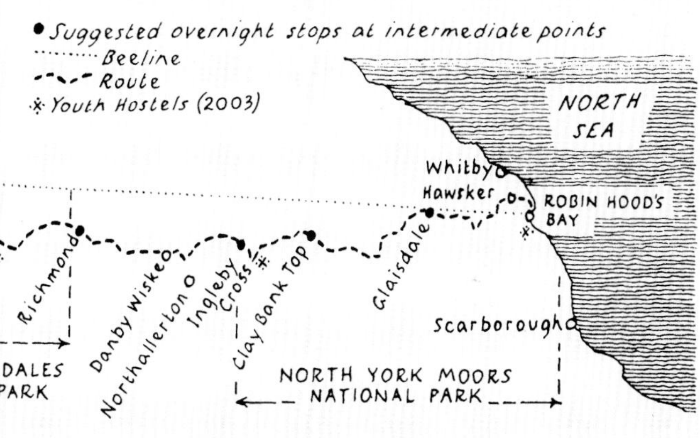

Patterdale and Shap)

feet
2000
1000

NATURAL FEATURES

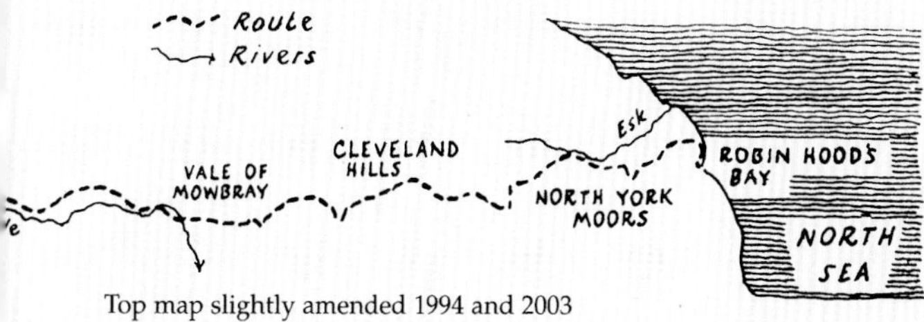

Top map slightly amended 1994 and 2003

ST BEES TO ROSTHWAITE

Julia's Overview

Here I was again, setting off into a bit of an unknown. The boots were on, the backpack was stuffed to the brim and I had a familiar friend for company. Only this time I only needed one little red guidebook, AW's *Coast to Coast Pictorial Guide.*

So far my walks with Wainwright had been simple; lovely, enticing rambling excursions into Lakeland, enchanting on occasion, exerting in places and uplifting in general. But most definitely day trips, albeit sometimes quite long days. This excursion however, presented a whole new ball game. This was long distance walking, a route of parts with a goal in the distance, the very distance.

So, as I ran down the pebbly beach at St Bees to mark the start of my journey by dipping my toes in the Irish Sea there was real exuberance in that dash to the water's edge.

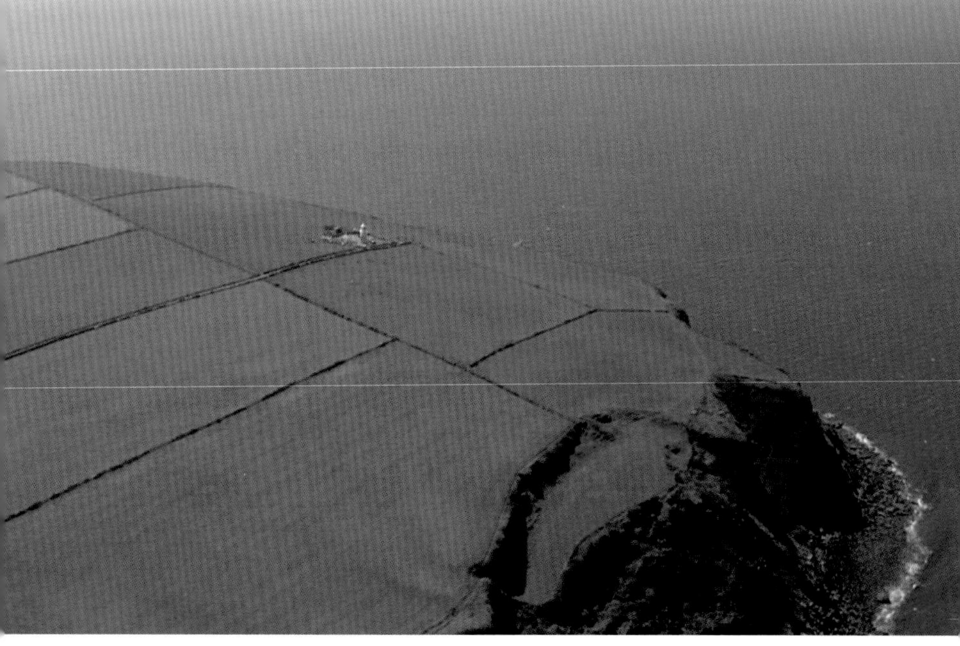

Aerial view of the St Bees lighthouse and the most westerly point on the Coast to Coast
Pages 18-19: South head, St Bees at dusk

This was the start of something entirely different for me. It was like the first day back at school, the bell had rung and it was time to muster; a whole new chapter in my walking explorations was about to unfold.

If I thought I'd experienced tiredness, batterings by the elements, navigational conundrums and chocolate induced sugar highs during my previous walks. It was all about to go up another notch. Eyes up, feet forward.

View from South Head, St. Bees, looking to Black Combe

THE WALK
GATEWAY TO THE LAKES
St Bees to Rosthwaite

DISTANCE: 29 miles/46.6 kilometres
St Bees to Ennerdale Bridge
14 ¼ miles/22.9 kilometres
Ennerdale Bridge to Rosthwaite
14.5 miles/23.3 kilometres
OS MAP: Explorer 303, OL4

OVERVIEW

Starting from the shores of the Irish Sea a full 4 miles (6.43 kilometres) of coastal footpath is followed by the flatlands and old mining villages of West Cumbria. The small foothill of Dent is a flavour of bigger things to come and leads into the most remote of all the Lake District valleys – Ennerdale. Here the Coast to Coast path hugs the edge of Ennerdale Water, taking a direct route up the valley, amongst some of the biggest peaks in the area. There's a steep climb passing around Wainwright's much loved peak, on Haystacks, across to Honister Pass and its very obvious slate mining. It's an industry, which has done much to shape the villages of this area and the lovely valley of Borrowdale, the destination for this first section.

The Walk

'The route follows an approximate beeline (if a beeline can ever be approximate) from one side of England to the other: from St Bees Head on the Irish Sea to Robin Hood's Bay on the North Sea and if a ruler is placed across a map between these two points it will be seen at a glance that the grandest territory in the north of England is traversed by it; indeed, two thirds of the route lies through the areas of three National Parks.'
A. Wainwright

An aerial view of the beach at St Bees and the start of the Coast to Coast route

Now, you really shouldn't start out on this walk until you've set foot on the beach itself. Once you are down on its shore there's a certain Coast to Coast tradition that you may like to follow. This involves choosing a pebble from this beach, popping it in your pocket and taking it with you all the way across northern England to your destination on the east coast. There's also something else that Wainwright advised. He didn't believe the walk had officially begun until you'd dipped your toes in the Irish Sea. This is no time to hold back, embrace that icy Irish Sea. My thinking is that this could actually aid the challenge you've set yourself, a bit of light refreshment for the toes may well sort of awaken them in readiness for the hard work that's ahead.

Once these traditions have been dutifully observed your Coast to Coast walk can get underway. Now, as well as walking & writing, Wainwright's other great contribution to his books was his drawing. Sketches abound, but just as valuable are his maps. Armed with your *Coast to Coast* guide you can see from a glance at his hand drawn map of the whole route what a comprehensive journey this is, marching its way between the two coasts. As Wainwright quickly realized, a straight line across northern England could include the Lake District, the Yorkshire Dales and the North York Moors, so three National Parks in one walk. From St Bees in the west to Robin Hood's Bay in the east, Wainwright certainly made 192 miles (308.9 kilometres) look incredibly simple.

So, if you tackle this journey as AW suggests, you will always be heading east. He recommended this direction because of the prevailing conditions, preferring to have the wind on his back rather than blowing in his face. He added:

Julia at St Bees

'In the case of this particular walk it is perhaps unfortunate that the grandest part of it, through Lakeland, comes so early, but those who do not already know the heather moors of north-east Yorkshire can be assured that they form a fitting climax.'

Don't be surprised that when you do start you will seem to be travelling in slightly the wrong direction. AW himself points out the walk does begin a little 'disconcertingly' by heading north along the cliffs.

'It is along the top of the cliffs, that this long journey to Robin Hood's Bay begins. There is no possibility of getting lost but there is a risk of accident on the seaward side of the fence: assurance of ultimately arriving at Robin Hood's Bay is much greater if the landward side is preferred.'

These cliffs have been the cause of concern since at least 1717 when a lighthouse was first installed on the tip of St Bees Head. This building however also marks the most westerly point on the Coast to Coast path.

It was at this spot that I had the pleasure of meeting up again with an old Lakeland acquaintance and the man who nearly twenty-five years ago accompanied Alfred Wainwright on one of his last television appearances. Eric Robson, broadcaster, writer and filmmaker had the rare privilege of joining AW to film a journey along his Coast to Coast route. 'It was like yesterday that I began this walk with AW. It was an adventure, an expedition, he was just enjoying himself. He was particularly fond and proud of the Coast to Coast walk.' However, Eric did reveal that despite AW's claims that one could do the walk in twelve days, he certainly never did. 'That runs counter to everything he suggests – he encourages walkers to take their time, to dawdle, to enjoy it. At the heart of his project was the notion that here was one suggestion, it was 'a' Coast to Coast walk not 'the' Coast to Coast walk. It was an adventure and an expedition, he wanted everybody to basically stick to his route but go and explore from it'.

St. Bees Lighthouse

I'd got to know Eric through my first real brush with Lakeland when I'd tackled ten of AW's classic routes for the first television series. Eric had advised me on places to go, and had even come out and encouraged me along on certain routes and checked in on me after I had returned. He was one of those wonderful warm and

Julia with Eric Robson at St Bees Head Lighthouse

welcoming local characters that were very much a part of my 'Lake District' so far. So, as I said farewell to him and asked him to wish me luck his reply reminded me just how far my Wainwright wanderings had already taken me. He simply said: 'You don't need luck, you're a seasoned, hardened walker now'. With the miles now stretching out ahead I realised I was about to become just a little bit more seasoned.

Leaving the lighthouse there's just the northern tip of St Bees Head to deal with before Wainwright allows you to say goodbye to the west coast. Finally you're on your way to the ultimate destination.

The thin ribbon of land stretched between the coast and the first national park is rarely mentioned by those recounting their Coast to Coast highlights. Instead it's been an industrial heartland for around 800 years. Where walkers are now welcomed, it was once Cornish tin miners who flocked to seek a new fortune and establish new communities. The first of these, Moor Row, now comprises fairly typical West Cumbrian cottages. It enjoyed a brief period of prosperity due to iron and coal.

Views back out to the Irish Sea from the first climb of the route at Dent

As you make your way through the village you should be able to pick out the railway line that used to service that industry. Wainwright lamented 'On the greyest of Cumbrian afternoons and with mining, chemicals and the railway all gone it's easy to see the opening stretch of the Coast to Coast as quite a sad environment.' But the final village of Cleator marks the start of a new chapter. The route from here provides a springboard into AW's beloved Lakeland and appropriately enough the start of the first real climb. Wainwright wrote: 'The green hill of Dent…is an excellent viewpoint, with a panorama far wider than its modest elevation would suggest…'

Now, industries have come and gone in these part but once you reach this first climb you will be able to spot one that still makes quite a big noise round here and that's Sellafield, the world's first nuclear power station. It's certainly quite a sight, but not necessarily for all the right reasons. On a clear day the Isle of Man can also be spotted. But it's probably the sight of what lies ahead that will fix your gaze. AW describes this moment only too well: 'on the ascent from the west it

Looking west towards Ennerdale Water on the route you have just followed

is the sudden revelation of the Lakeland fells that rivets the attention, the prospect being unexpectedly good.'

From up here you can certainly enjoy a brief moment of satisfaction, the Irish Sea is behind you, there will be some mud on your boots and you've got your first little peak under your belt. The joys of walking certainly come flooding back once you're away from the towns and roads and with the prospect of the Lake District ahead, I think you're allowed to revel in a small feeling of excitement.

Whether it was with luck or skill, Wainwright found a path into Lakeland that followed the quietest of all routes, the seemingly secret valley of Nannycatch. AW described it fondly as an 'Arcadia-in-miniature', ' a charming place' and 'a shyly hidden ravine'. But the niftily named Nannycatch Gate also marks a boundary, this is where you step into the Lake District National Park for the first time.

From here, Ennerdale Bridge is the next goal, the first Lakeland village and the final destination for most walkers, after what can seem a pretty gruelling first day. But a tantalising view of things to come may well help to keep

Julia at Ennerdale Water

those tired legs moving. AW's joy at being reunited with his beloved fells is clear: 'As Ennerdale Bridge is approached, an exciting array of impressive mountains comes into view to the east, encircling the long deep valley of Ennerdale. Now, we really are on the threshold of Lakeland…'

For any walker this next section should be a real treat. Some of the biggest peaks in the country await. Ennerdale Bridge stands just a mile from the first lake of this 'Lakeland' section. AW describes it with clear affection: 'Ennerdale Water, most westerly of the Lakes, is remote from the usual haunts

Ennerdale Bridge

Ennerdale Bridge is a convenient halting place at the end of the first day. It is a quiet hamlet, known to west Cumbrians but not to the general Lakes tourist. Nevertheless a choice of lodging is to be found in or around the village, including hotels and bed-and-breakfast accommodation. There is also a bunk house at Low Cock How. *(Turn left 300 yards north of Kinniside Stone Circle.)*

Ennerdale Water and Pillar

of Lakeland's visitors, yet it lies in a pleasantly rural setting at the outlet of a valley deeply inurned between lofty mountain ranges of which the view across the water is splendid, and in evening sunlight supremely beautiful.'

When I made the accompanying TV series to this book we were able to include some of the original BBC footage showing AW en route. On reaching Ennerdale Water he recounted the rather comic tale of the Angler's Hotel, which used to be situated on the lake's edge, recollecting that you could fish right from the hotel, out of the window, into the water. I'm afraid there's no longer such distraction to keep

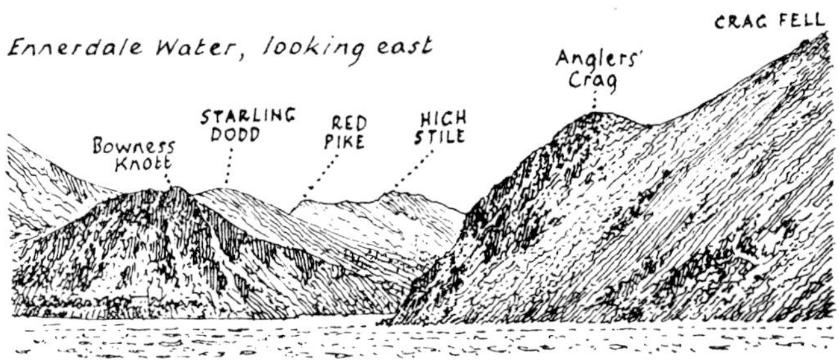

you from the walk ahead. Ennerdale Water however, serves as a special gateway to the Lakes, this is the point where coastal lowlands turn into two thousand foot peaks.

As you make your way along the southern edge of Ennerdale Water you will reach Angler's Crag, where a rocky outcrop can be spotted. Wainwright writes 'old maps show this as Robin Hood's Chair', and although the name has gone out of use, it seems appropriate to revive it because of its affinity with our ultimate objective: his Bay.' At this stage however the prospect of Robin Hood's Bay may seem an entirely distant one.

Apart from the sheep, walkers enjoy a complete monopoly around Ennerdale Water. It is the only major lake in the area without a road. But with iron ore, charcoal burning, farming and forestry, this quietest of valleys has actually been carefully managed by mankind since the Iron Age. Today however, a project called 'Wild Ennerdale' is deliberately attempting to let nature take control. If a tree falls, it is left to rot contributing to one of the longest running wild land restoration projects in the UK. Here, the landscape is encouraged to evolve naturally by reducing human intervention.

As the route heads further into the Ennerdale Forest it also skirts alongside the River Liza. AW describes the power of this mountain born torrent: 'In dry seasons a wide channel of boulders scoured from the rocky fastness at the head of Ennerdale and then rounded and bleached by sun and water, but hidden below a tumultuous cataract in time of spate.' You can certainly peer into its watery depths as you make your way across the forestry bridge, which AW sketched and included in his guidebook.

As Wainwright himself says 'all things come to an end' and the cloaking green of Ennerdale Forest eventually gives way, rather 'like coming out of a dark room into sunlight.' The upper end of this valley then leads to one of my favourite spots, a sudden outpost of humanity in the midst of an increasingly wilder and wilder landscape.

When Wainwright describes the Black Sail Youth Hostel in his *Coast to Coast* guide he captures its splendid isolated position perfectly. 'Black Sail Hut is the loneliest and most romantic of youth hostels, situated in a magnificent surround of mountainous country. Great Gable dominates the head of the valley with Green Gable and Kirk Fell in support; looking back, Pillar is seen soaring above the forest, and High Crag and Haystacks form an impressive wall to the north.' It's a sumptuous view indeed, one that will fulfil a walker's desire for lofty mountaintops. 'Why go to Switzerland?' wrote AW (well, apart for the chocolate I couldn't agree more).

The last time I came to this youth hostel I was heading up Pillar, filming for my BBC *Wainwright Walks* series. It was the final walk of the series and it felt like I had reached a kind of pinnacle in my Wainwright wanderings. It was also the biggest challenge I'd faced, in attempting to follow in the

An aerial view of the well-worn path leading towards Honister where ponies once carried wagons laden with slate

footsteps of the great man. But here I was again, same spot, but this time a different route and what felt like another pretty daunting challenge.

Leaving the youth hostel you meet with a rather more unusual sight as the fellside starts to roll in great wave-like undulations. These distinctive egg-shaped mounds are in fact drumlins, left behind by a melting glacier. This striking geological reference is another reminder of just how far removed this valley feels. Here, it is just you, the elements and this raw and rugged landscape for company. AW describes some of that drama: 'The glacier tore away from its moorings on Great Gable at the end of the Ice Age and shuffled down to the sea leaving evidence of its slow journey along the valley. The forest hides many traces but plain to see at the open dalehead are stranded boulders, ice-scratched and polished rocks and a wide area of drumlins, the latter, looking like giant anthills.'

It was that same glacier that left behind the next challenge, the steep sidewall of the valley. Loft Beck provides one of the

Julia with John Taylor at Honister Slate Mine

few accessible routes out of Ennerdale. This is quite possibly the steepest quarter-mile on the entire Coast to Coast walk, so it's quite nice to get it out of the way so early on in the route. As you climb out its 'goodbye' Ennerdale and 'hello' Borrowdale.

The reward for reaching the top of the beck is a majestic high-level walk. It's also a good spot to admire your handiwork and look back at what you've achieved. To the west lies the whole of your walk, right back to Ennerdale Bridge. To the north is a view over Buttermere to Crummock Water.

A well-marked path now follows. This is where ponies would have carried slate over the fells and back out to the west coast. The ponies may have gone but as you approach the Honister Pass, modern signs of the Lakeland slate industry are obvious. At the point AW marked as Drum House you can pick out the straight path where horses would have pulled wagons full of slate where a gravity system would have then lowered these loads into the pass below. From up here you also get a glimpse into Borrowdale, the final goal for this section of the walk.

But before you can reach journey's end for the day each

and every Coast to Coast walker is funnelled through the hub of the age-old local industry. Unlike the hateful conifers of Ennerdale, Wainwright was enamoured with the sheer history of the Honister slate story, and equally saddened on his last visit by what appeared to be its demise.

During the making of his TV *Coast to Coast* programme in 1989, he was saddened to find a deserted quarry, boarded up, and devoid of all human activity. Centuries of Lakeland history appeared to have come to an end. AW had lamented: 'Men laboured for all their lives on the crag. And now, it's just like a graveyard.'

It's an entirely different scene, which greets you as you head this way today. Honister is up and running once again. In the late 1990s the dilapidated site was bought by a Borrowdale lad, Mark Weir, who set about exploiting whatever local expertise he could muster. He started by recruiting a true old hand, his own uncle, John Taylor.

One of the great things about my television work is the people I get to meet and the lives I get to glimpse into. Some might only be fleeting moments, a chance conversation struck up on a fellside path, whilst others sometimes turn into something else. Meeting Mark Weir was definitely one of those. This insatiably enthusiastic man was more than a filming acquaintance, a true friend, and so it was with enormous sadness that we learned of his tragic death in 2011 after a fatal helicopter accident. It feels therefore only right and proper to mention him here because he was the force behind Hoinster's revival. He wanted to breath life back into this special spot and took so many strides towards achieving this. I suspect AW would have been heartened to see life return to the slate mine he too loved. I not only had the pleasure of meeting Mark on many occasions but I also got to interview his Uncle, a wonderfully warm man who clearly loved his job. 'It's beautiful. Underground is a different world. You forget everything, especially working among good rock. This is the best grey slate country'.

Having passed so many lost industries already, it's nice

to find one that's enjoying renewed success. Today Honister is both a traditional industry but also a visitor attraction for walkers and coach-parties alike. There are underground tours of the slate mines as well as a rather more unusual *via ferrata* excursion following in the footsteps of the miners along their original cliff-edge footpath high on Fleetwith Pike.

From Honister the route winds gently into Borrowdale. As AW said, the Lake District is the loveliest part of England, and this, its fairest valley. Making your way to Rosthwaite is a gentle indulgence in all those soft charms of Lakeland. AW captured it well: 'The picture as a whole is entirely delightful: scenically it is informal to the point of untidiness, yet all things blend in perfect harmony. Man and Nature, working together have made a good job of Borrowdale.'

There's still a long, long way to go... but by this stage you will have some miles under your belt and you might just be starting to feel like you are a proper Coast to Coaster.

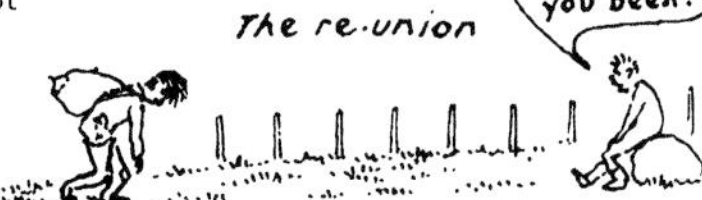

Borrowdale
Left: An aerial view of Borrowdale, which AW described as the 'fairest' of Lakelands valleys

Tears and Triumphs

Highlights: A sunset to savour over Ennerdale Water and a possible 'Haribo' induced sugar rush.

Lowpoint: Rain halts play for quite a few hours. I had to get a right old wriggle on to chalk up the remaining mileage.

ROSTHWAITE TO SHAP

Julia's Overview

This next chapter of the book refers to what was for me, a very special part of a Coast to Coast walk. This was going to take me through true Wainwright country, crossing the heart of the Lakes. Journeying through such iconic landscapes felt like it would be an achievement in itself, after all, here was a route laying out some of the best of Lakeland, as well as taking me to the highest point of the Coast to Coast path.

Until embarking on a Coast to Coast walk my Lakeland wanderings really had only ever been single days, or a couple at most, with summits gained and peaks explored. Rosthwaite to Shap lay down a new gauntlet for me. It was some familiar fellwandering, through territory I knew and had begun to love, with the added challenge of distance thrown in.

Get to the end of this section at Shap and you have already achieved something quite remarkable – a march across Wainwright's beloved Lakeland…okay so there's the small matter of the rest of England to contend with afterwards. But that can wait. For the next few days Lakeland is your unfolding backdrop and you can simply indulge yourself in some of Wainwright's 'heavenly' home turf. You're feeling it in your boots by now.

Haweswater and High Street from the old Corpse Road to Shap
Pages 40-41: The view west past Hayeswater from High Street summit plateau

The head of Ullswater

THE WALK

HEART OF THE LAKES

Rosthwaite to Shap

DISTANCE: 34 miles/54.7 kilometres
OS MAP: OL 4 & 5

OVERVIEW

An immediate ridge of high ground takes you almost due south out of Rosthwaite, to find a high-level escape from Borrowdale, over Greenup Edge. The route then passes into Easedale. You descend almost as far as Grasmere before climbing again to pass between the giant peaks of Helvellyn and Fairfield. You will then pass through Griesdale and down to the village of Patterdale at the southern foot of Ullswater. From here, the final Lakeland chapter takes you to the very roof of the Coast to Coast path – Kidsty Pike. The final stretch through Lakeland takes you along the length of Haweswater and across open farmland to the town of Shap.

The Walk

'It is a country walk of the sort that enthusiasts for the hills and open spaces indulge in every weekend. It's a bit longer than most, that's all.'
A. Wainwright

An aerial view of the charming Lakeland village of Rosthwaite

Starting out from Rosthwaite you can't help but feel you are getting close to the heart of the Lake District. Only 29 miles (46.6 kilometres) in and already the route seems a world away from those flatland beginnings by the Irish Sea. This next bit of the Coast to Coast walk will take you towards some of the highest land in England and true Wainwright country.

Whilst this pretty little Lakeland village will feel like a quiet little bolthole it is also known as the capital of Borrowdale. With its rambling stone cottages and twisty little lanes it's certainly no metropolis, but in these parts this is a hub. Even on a wet day, this corner of Cumbria can throng with walkers, all drawn here for the same reason as Alfred Wainwright. There's no doubt in my mind that this would have been one of the most eagerly anticipated sections of the walk for AW. Not only are you about to reach the highest point on the entire Coast to Coast walk but there's tough fell trampling up ahead as well. So for Wainwright this section threw him a challenge; to find the best possible route through the best possible landscape. This was, after all, his beloved and favoured stomping ground. He wrote of the fells: 'Surely there is no other place in this whole wonderful world quite like Lakeland...no other so exquisitely lovely, no other so charming. All who truly love Lakeland are exiles when away from it.'

The Coast to Coast walk very deliberately takes in three national parks as it heads from sea to sea. But no other section of the route is so devoted to exploring the beauty and nature of one of those parks as this one. Whether it takes you two days, three days or even longer, the stretch from Rosthwaite to Shap is a grand traverse of some of the greatest lines of English mountains.

Wainwright was possibly Rosthwaite's biggest fan and said that the climb out of the village was a 'walk in heaven'. Unfortunately as I prepared to step out on the start of my grand trek out of Borrowdale and across the middle of the Lakes it looked like it would be a very wet and misty walk in heaven.

A bit of rain is one thing, but with the route to Grasmere lost in the cloud and with a film crew to worry about, even the best navigator would be foolhardy to roam the higher ground on a morning such as ours.

Sometimes, you just have to accept the inevitable and wait for things to improve, something that AW was only too happy to do when, twenty years ago, he invited Eric Robson and a TV crew to join him along his Coast to Coast walk. They too holed up and waited for the rain to pass, sipping cups of tea. As I had started to learn on my previous Wainwright walks, sometimes you just have to sit it out. Wainwright himself was famous for carefully selecting the days that he ventured out to explore the fells. But then again, he did live

An aerial view of Griesdale Tarn, reached after leaving Grasmere

in Kendal, on the doorstep of the Lakes. For those of us who travel far for cherished weekends & the odd holiday amongst the fells, there's an urge to get out at the first sign of any improvement.

Once you do get back out then of course you have to look on the bright side, all that rain does liven up the surroundings, guaranteeing bulging rivers and gushing waterfalls. When planning my Coast to Coast walk, I opted for September, often regarded as the best month of all for walking in northern England. But little did I know that the preceding August would be the wettest in a long time. September appeared to then follow a similar course. So, our filming was challenging, to say the least, and unfortunately what should have been a rather dramatic and uplifting bit of fellwandering on this first section of my route was a bit of a wash out. Lakeland paths were fast turning into streams, camera lenses were misting, boots were filling, and research notes were turning to mush.

Making it to Grasmere did feel like arriving at a bit of sanctuary, a bolthole out of the elements where we could take solace with a hot drink and I think on this occasion

An aerial view over Ullswater
Right: Julia in Grisedale

probably a few restorative buns. It's a place I'd been to many times before along with tens of thousands of other people. Wainwright once described Grasmere as 'a lovely village... with sylvan grace and dignity.' One of its rather famous residents, Lakeland poet William Wordsworth, called this his 'beloved vale'. This was of course praise enough to attract visitors in their droves. With the rather noisy and always seemingly busy A591 now transporting visitors into the heart of this Lakeland scene Grasmere is definitely 'easy access'. But you don't have to put up with the interruption of traffic for too long. This road is your cue for the next leg of the journey and from here you head into the area Wainwright knew as the Eastern Fells.

The next section of the Coast to Coast walk crosses the southern end of the Helvellyn Range, past the amphitheatre-like Grisedale Tarn. The Tarn is a real mountain crossroads, not only the passing point between two great valleys, but an access for peaks like Fairfield, St Sunday Crag and the ever popular Helvellyn. But for Coast to Coast walkers, this is the

route to one of England's great lakes, lauded by Wainwright and loved by thousands more. Ullswater's size and setting seems to ensure that its beauty is never compromised.

Unfortunately for me, conditions during my walk continued to provide a bit of a battering. By the time I approached the lake it was like I'd been in a permanent wind tunnel. Funnily enough though, the last time I had been in this vicinity, I was heading in the opposite direction towards the very top of Helvellyn and the weather was pretty much the same… awful. But somewhere deep down, there's something about wet days in the Lakes that I think you begin to love. Once you accept the wet boots, and the water running down your nose, there's still an immense beauty to be appreciated on these days. It somehow becomes part of the walker's lot, you learn to take the rough with the smooth.

Wainwright recommends that you do this walk west to east, because five days out of six the wind is in your favour. This must have been the 'off' day as I had the wind right in my face, along with the rain. But the need for a little bit of respite from that rain did help me step that bit closer to AW. As you walk down from Griesdale Tarn, passing Ruthwaite Lodge and down towards Patterdale you will eventually see

The stone barn, which AW sheltered in overnight on Coronation Day, 1953

a sturdy stone barn, a place that Wainwright himself used for shelter.

When AW retraced his steps for his own *Coast to Coast* TV series he brought Eric Robson to this spot. The first time he had been there it was Coronation Day, a public holiday, and in typical AW fashion he had been in the hills. Making the most of the time off he'd stayed out late and then sought shelter in this barn overnight. But worried that he'd not had permission from the farmer he'd been up at the crack of dawn to get the first bus home from Grasmere. AW returned back to work that morning to discover Everest had been summited by Edmund Hillary and Tenzing Norgay. So whilst it might have been a rough night's sleep it was somewhere AW remembered well, reminiscing: 'It pricked a bubble for me as I'd always had the impossible ambition to be the first man on Everest, so it's a day I remember.'

As you reach the bottom end of Grisedale the rough open fell gives way to cultivated fields and the valley curves to meet the southern end of Ullswater. But the target is Patterdale, the village that was the start point for my previously rain

An aerial view down to Ullswater and Patterdale

drenched climb up Helvellyn. Wainwright considered this a spot that could rival Borrowdale 'in the magnificence of its surroundings.' The view, as AW suggests, lays the best of Lakeland out before you. 'With crags and heathery fells rising from a strath of emerald valley pastures and a wealth of noble trees, the scene is one of informal but exquisite beauty.' It's certainly a welcome sight for any walker who, like me, has

Ullswater, from the north-east ridge of St. Sunday Crag

been buffeted, battered and beaten by inhospitable mountain weather.

Still quiet and charming, with no sprawling developments, I suspect Wainwright would have been chuffed to find Patterdale almost as he left it. Just as in his day this lovely village, which AW described as 'truly Alpine in situation', is still opening its doors to tired and hungry walkers in search of a bed for the night. But before you shed your walking boots for the day Wainwright offers one last bit of advice that's still well worth heeding: '... take a stroll across the valley to the lakeside path below Place Fell for a view of Ullswater that is unsurpassed for loveliness.'

If you do make time to explore Patterdale one of the lovely things you will find is the village shop. It's one of those cavernous places that seems to have everything from ice creams to woolly socks, as well a very good selection of books. This is in fact the shop where Wainwright first sold his guidebooks. Back in the 1950s when his books were first published he painstakingly went round shops himself trying to sell them. He came to this shop first whilst staying at a B&B down the road.

Patterdale is a great place to get some much-needed rest before the final day's walking in Lakeland. You might even like to discover the B&B that was Wainwright's chosen overnight spot. In those days Old Water View was known as Ullswater View, a name that lasted until a shroud of trees made the name less than appropriate. Adverts from the 1940s described the Ullswater View as 'a commodious house with all modern improvements...wired up with electric light', so clearly all mod cons back then.

Julia on top of Kidsty Pike

If you do happen to stay here you will be able to spot AW's familiar handwriting listing Mr & Mrs Wainwright and a Peter Wainwright. So almost thirty years before the *Coast to Coast* was published, the normally solitary Wainwright was here on what must have been a very rare trip to the Lakes with his first wife Ruth. From his bedroom window, AW would have been able to plot the first couple of miles of his final Lakeland chapter. It's a 19-mile (30.5-kilometre) monster that starts with a very big climb.

So, as you wind a route out of Patterdale you'll get one last glimpse of this picturesque Lakeland village. But there's no time to dillydally, this section of the Coast to Coast walk is going to put up quite a challenge. There's now the small

matter of a 2,500-foot (762-metre) peak to conquer. AW was however, rather more mournful about what lay ahead because in this section you will reach the final eastern edge of his beloved Lakeland.

He wrote: 'The journey from Patterdale to Shap involves a lofty crossing of the High Street massif, the final mountain barrier of Lakeland in the east, and during the course of the walk the scenery changes dramatically, sombre fells giving place to a pastoral limestone landscape. This is farewell to Lakeland and farewells to Lakeland are always sad.

What follows is a steady trek to the top of Kidsty Pike. It's 5 miles (8 kilometres) of uphill effort, that will certainly get the legs going, but the climb can be conveniently broken by a brief rest at the very obvious Angle Tarn, which AW described as 'an attractive sheet of water.' Many tarns appear as plugholes at the bottom of great basins in the hills. Angle Tarn however occupies a natural shelf and makes for a great platform looking west.

This is however, a famously exposed area of the Lakes. Here a succession of rolling whaleback summits means that there are few crags or cliffs to block the elements. At the very top is another of Wainwright's classics, High Street, named after the road once built by Roman soldiers to carry them across this inhospitable landscape. Even in his *Coast to Coast* guide AW mentions its delights: 'High Street is massively attractive, its Roman Road showing clearly, and its summit is easily reached from here.' Although he warns: 'if the hour is already past noon there really isn't time to do it.' He recommends taking the path branching over Twopenny Crag ('named pre-decimalisation'), which skirts the rim of Riggindale and leads on to Kidsty Pike.

Reaching Kidsty Peak is a milestone because this is the highest point of the Coast to Coast walk. Sadly, from here, even on a clear day, you can't see either coast. But there is still a real sense of satisfaction and it's a moment you should soak up because it's your last real view over Wainwright's favoured fells. As AW notes: 'its summit is the best station for taking a last long look at the serrated mountain skyline of Lakeland, the like of which will not be seen again this side of the North Sea. But there will be other years, other visits... The hills will wait.'

As you start to descend the broad grassy slopes off the summit you gain an ever-increasing view into one of Lakeland's quieter valleys. This last descent is a bit of a thigh burner but it is the most direct route down taking you along the spine of Kidsty Pike and straight to the shores of Haweswater. This ridge would have once led to the old valley of Mardale and into the lands of Riggindale Farm. But these are now long

forgotten landmarks, wiped away when Haweswater Lake was engulfed by Haweswater Reservoir in 1930.

When AW revisited the area he lamented these losses saying there was 'Nothing like the romantic charm of the old valley.' He described how there would have been 'green pastures, farmhouses fringed with birches and little beaches where the cows would come and stand.'

Today, the Haweswater Dam is a pretty unmissable landmark, which signals you are back down on the valley floor and about to leave the rolling fells of Lakeland far behind. From 1929 onwards, two hundred men set up a base here to construct this 98-foot high wall (30-metre). Just like the dam itself the bungalows they left behind are still going strong.

This might well be more than can be said for your legs at this stage. As you come close to the end of this toughest of sections, you can think back to the climbs, scrambles (and certainly, in my case, the weather). Already you have notched up quite an achievement. You can now make the bold claim to have walked right across the Lake District, from the flatlands of West Cumbria, to the rolling farmlands at the edge of the Eden Valley.

Rolling flatlands lead from Haweswater to Shap

The town of Shap is the final goal but a more evocative sight are the ruins of Shap Abbey, the very last abbey to be founded in England and also the last to be closed down by Henry VIII. It is both an entrance to the town and the point at which you leave your first National Park.

You might well breathe a sigh of relief as you head down Kidsty Pike, but then you've got the length of Haweswater to go and this final push to Shap. So it's goodbye to the Lake District, and goodbye to Wainwright country. Now, some people think that the Lakes should be the cherry at the end of the Coast to Coast walk. Personally, I really enjoyed walking through Wainwright's Lakeland, it felt like a major accomplishment and something that would fuel me along the rest of my journey.

But just in case the efforts of the last few days leave you questioning whether this journey is for you or not I'll leave you with some of AW's sage words. At this stage they may just be what you need to hear.

The ruins of Shap Abbey, the very last abbey to be founded in England

'Well it's not too late to abandon the Coast to Coast idea and stay in Patterdale. There is nothing ahead as good – admittedly... Anyway, please yourself, stay if you want to. And let's be clear about this – you can't expect to get your money back for the book if you prefer not to continue... coming with me? Good. I thought you would.'

Tears and Triumphs

Highlights: Lakeland, Lakeland, Lakeland... Treading familiar ground with good old AW for company. The flapjack we cracked open atop Kidsty Pike has never tasted so good. I swear it's the Lakeland air.

Lowpoint: I arrived on the shores of Ullswater with hair slicked and slapped across the face having received a natural facial exfoliation from the elements. It was a windy day in Wainwright world.

SHAP TO KELD

Julia's Overview

I think it was during this leg of the journey that I felt I turned into a long-distance walker. Up until this point the route had taken me through familiar territory. I'd been as absorbed as ever by Wainwright's Lakeland, comfortable in the knowledge that I knew this place and felt at ease in this landscape of fells and lakes. I felt I understood what Wainwright was all about in these places because I'd already had the opportunity to explore some of his fells and lofty summits for my previous TV series.

But Lakeland was gone and whilst I knew this was a cross-country route when I embarked on it I think it really dawned on me as we left the Lakes behind. We were going further than ever before, for longer than before. Day after day I'd be walking –not just snagging the glory of another peak.

Trudging through mud can have a sobering effect and the Pennines certainly threw that at us. So I think I turned a corner in this section. I went from being someone who

Julia crossing the Pennines
Left: Upper Lune Valley near Orton
Pages 62-63: Faraday Gill en route to Nine Standards

relished a good old summit height to being a walker focussed on chalking up the miles, each evening diligently totting up the distance travelled each day. And it's fair to say that by the end of this section I positively revelled in the realisation that we were already half-way across England. All that mud trudging and bean counting was worth it in the end.

Kirkby Stephen

top:

The Parish Church of St. Stephen

bottom:

Frank's Bridge

THE WALK
EDEN & THE PENNINES
Shap to Keld

DISTANCE: Shap to Kirkby Stephen 20 miles/32.1 kilometres
Kirkby Stephen to Keld 12 ¾ miles/20.5 kilometres
OS MAP: OL5 &19

OVERVIEW

Leaving Shap you first have to cross the West Coast Main Line and the M6 motorway to set foot on the Limestone plateau of the Eden Valley. It's then time for something rather more rough underfoot as you cross heather and bracken as the route leads beneath a line of rocky scars overlooking Orton village. You will then cross the Scandal Beck at Smardale Bridge, before reaching the first major town at Kirkby Stephen. The town marks the start of the Pennines, which means a long climb to the Coast to Coast path's natural watershed at the remarkable Nine Standards Rigg. From there, it's a descent through peat bogs and moorland into the quiet delights of upper Swaledale, and the tiny village of Keld. At this point you will have walked halfway across the country.

The Walk

'Surely there cannot be a finer itinerary for a long-distance walk! For sustained beauty, variety and interest it puts the Pennine Way to shame.'
A. Wainwright

An aerial view approaching Kirkby Stephen at the end of your stretch along the Eden Valley

Stretched along one of the highest main roads in Britain, Shap is a name better known to motorists than walkers. But for followers of Alfred Wainwright, this is the start of the next Coast to Coast chapter. Already you will have crossed the whole of the Lake District, striding through some of England's greatest mountain ranges in order to stand here, ready to explore a very different landscape. The first section of the walk through the Lake District is pretty hardcore so you may be glad to hear that this next section is certainly easier terrain. But it's also the land of mystery and ancient remains. So, whilst we're moving into unchartered water, there's still plenty to look forward to.

Heading east out of Shap, there's a sparse but fascinating world waiting and one considerably less documented than previous parts of the walk. Lying between the Lakes and the Yorkshire Dales on Wainwright's Coast to Coast route, stands a stretch of northern England known as the Eden Valley. This is a broad, undulating corridor running from Shap to Kirkby Stephen. From there the Pennines take over, leading up and over into the upper reaches of Swaledale.

What lies waiting at this journey's end is a far cry from the initial first strides of the day. At this point the environment probably couldn't feel more different, as you do battle to hear yourself over the racing din of the M6 motorway. Confronting something like this is of course a bit of a jolt. It's always such a shock when a road like this pops up on what's meant to be an idyllic walk. But there's a footbridge, so very quickly you can navigate your way up and over and then let the walk really begin.

The character of the walk changes completely and as

Julia takes a moment to soak up the view from Oddendale stone circle (a brief detour recommended by AW)

AW suggests there's plenty to look forward to: 'The terrain between Shap and Kirkby Stephen takes the form of a limestone plateau…And as every walker knows, a limestone footing, invariably means easy travelling on velvet turf, especially when the rock is outcropping or just below the surface, while its appearance when exposed to weather – crinkled, fissured and often grotesquely sculptured – allied to its glittering whiteness in sunlight, is of course a delight to the eye always.'

As you make your way towards Oddendale you may well start to see a few boulders, looking like they have been liberally scattered at the wayside. The answer for this lies in glaciation. The last Ice Age, saw thousands of granite boulders pushed, dragged and deposited here by sheets of ice and then left to rest on a bed of new limestone. Root around a little more and you may be able to find the remnants of a stone circle. It's not necessarily easy to find, Oddendale is clearly no Stonehenge, but this was one of Wainwright's preferred locations to sit and take a moment.

When AW retraced his steps he brought Eric Robson back to this spot explaining it was the only one of its kind that he'd ever seen. It also provides a pretty nifty spot for looking out across the entire Eden Valley.

With the roar of the M6 now far behind, you can really start to appreciate the area which AW and fellow traditionalists will always know as Westmorland. The Eden Valley was a key part of this historic county, which stretched from Lake Windermere in the west, to the Pennines in the east until 1974, when the whole county was absorbed into the new county of Cumbria.

As the outline of the Pennines start to loom large you can certainly enjoy a growing sense of space, freedom and emptiness and the feeling that you have the place to yourself. As Wainwright's maps suggest, this is an area where the population has declined over centuries, from ancient settlements and burial grounds, to disused limekilns and dismantled railways. When Wainwright devised his Coast to Coast walk, one of his objectives was to avoid towns. He certainly managed it because during the entire walk you only pass through two. This next spot, Kirkby Stephen, a veritable metropolis given your previous surroundings, is the first.

The town might still be quite compact but in this part of the world, its influence covers a wide rural area. After days of fells, lakes and valleys, it's very obvious you've arrived in a place where walkers are not the only traffic passing through. This is a community largely unaffected by visitors where centuries of market town tradition happily continue.

Before anyone leaves this welcome civilization it would be silly not to make proper use of at least some of the facilities.

An aerial view of the remarkable Nine Standards Rigg, which also marks the watershed of the Pennines

Wainwright aficionados are in no doubt as to what the man's favourite meal was. AW claimed that fish & chips formed his staple diet for eighty years. When you've got the Pennine peaks to conquer in the morning, you can't feel too guilty about enjoying a serious plate-full at the appropriately name 'Coast to Coast' chippy.

The next day's walk from Kirkby Stephen is one of the key moments on the Coast to Coast route. The map may look almost devoid of features but that's only because there's 13 miles (20.9 kilometres) of mountain, moor and bog to be negotiated. The Pennines are a real landmark though because this marks the point at which you stop walking away from the west coast, and start walking towards the east coast.

The Yorkshire valley of Swaledale is the next goal, but on the way stands one of the great ancient mysteries of these mountains. AW wrote: 'There are many theories about the origin of the group of cairns long known as the Nine Standards. Certainly they are very old, appearing on eighteenth-century

Julia explores the mysterious Nine Standards Rigg

maps and giving their name to the hill they adorn. They have multiplied slowly, visitors in more recent times having added a few more.'

At this stage, the Eden Valley will be fading into the background, or the mist if you have a day anything like mine, and it's back to Wainwright's favoured higher grounds. For almost 5 miles (8 kilometres), the top of the Pennines is a clear and constant target. The tiny outlines of Nine Standards slowly grow larger on an otherwise bare horizon.

They are certainly a rather intriguing addition to this part of the route and AW reflects further on their appearance: 'They occupy a commanding position overlooking the Eden

The aerial view over the Eden Valley, an area that was once part of the historic county, Westmorland, which stretched from Lake Windermere in the east to the Pennines in the west

Valley, this giving rise to the legend that they were built to give the marauding Scots the impression that an English army was encamped here. More likely they were boundary cairns (the county boundary formerly passed through them), or beacons. Harder to believe is the theory that the builder's were local lads with nothing better to do to pass their time. Whatever their purpose, they were meant to endure, having suffered little from the storms of centuries.'

As you approach the Nine Standards summit, the Coast to Coast route surpasses the 2,000 foot (609.6 metres) mark for only the second time. Without the competition of so many Lakeland Fells, the view here is the most extensive of the whole walk.

When you do actually get up close and personal with these bizarre beacons you can't help but be intrigued even more. Since leaving the Lakes you will have passed a stone circle and ancient remains, but there hasn't been anything quite like this. They are impressive up close, these strange,

Julia on the Pennines with Nine Standards in the background

enigmatic, mysterious lumps. But who would go to this trouble here in the middle of nowhere and why?

Recent research has produced a few scant answers to the mystery of the nine great cairns. They are believed to be at least two hundred years old, but could be as much as a thousand. Whether they are meant to honour a saint, repel armies or simply mark a county boundary is something future generations will continue to argue.

But perhaps more than any point, save for the very end of the walk, Nine Standards is a cause for celebration. This is the watershed for the entire Coast to Coast walk because up until now you've been walking against the flow of rivers and streams. As AW points out you are also rewarded with 'the most extensive and interesting viewpoint.' Over to the southeast he describes 'the promised land of Swaledale' and advises: 'Somewhere in that haze is the foot of our personal rainbow, journey's end. If you are carrying a can of beer prepare to drink it now.'

An aerial view of the Whitsundale Beck, which winds its way down to the lower reaches of Birkdale

But this next section of the route can certainly be one that you have to steel yourself for. There's a vast moor-top landscape, with hidden streams and acres of leg sapping bog and completely out of sight of all human habitation. This is not a terrain that should be tackled lightly, but it's one that thousands of Coast to Coast walkers struggle across each year. For such a mammoth walk, that crosses three national parks, it actually only encompasses two counties, Cumbria and Yorkshire. For keen navigators there will be a point where you can quite precisely place a foot in each, and you might as well have a bit of fun in the mud, there's not much else I can recommend about it (and a bit of bog and county straddling will make a good photo).

This is also the boundary of the Yorkshire Dales National Park, a delicate environment of fragile peat bog, where walkers are channelled along one of three different routes. My walk followed the 'blue' route, used, believe it or not

Crossing the River Swale, your companion for the next 50 miles, or so, to Richmond and beyond

for those dry days of early autumn. But, after an incredibly wet summer, the odd wooden stake was about the only thing reminding me that I wasn't just plodding through a neverending mudbath.

I'm sure Wainwright would have reluctantly accepted the need to prescribe routes for his many followers here. The next section heads along the Whitsundale Beck, a secluded and much-admired valley for Wainwright with endless spurs, meanders and overhangs. There's a definite drama here which AW keenly captured: 'The valley of Whitsundale bisects an upland wilderness east of Nine Standards Rigg and winds its way down into the lower reaches of Birkdale. It is of considerable size and yet little known and rarely visited: it is deeply enclosed by moors, is unseen from usual pedestrian tracks and unsuspected from the only motor road in the vicinity. A few farms occupy the entrance to the valley but beyond Raven Seat all is desolation profound.'

Kirkby Stephen

It's been a whole 9 miles (14.4 kilometres) since your last encounter with civilization but this next section brings you alongside the next bit of cultivated land, at the very tip of Swaledale. The farm at Raven Seat is the first outpost of humanity, a sure sign that your Pennine crossing is almost at an end. On my walk there was some light relief too, after all the squelching, in the form of a rather nice cream tea. The scones were freshly made and the tea piping hot, a small consolation for the efforts of the last few hours. Amanda Owen, who runs the farm with her husband also manages to combine being shepherdess, farmhand and mum of four with early morning baking sprees (and I thought what I'd been doing was tiring).

Leaving Raven Seat AW advises: 'Pleasant walking

Kirkby Stephen's main street

follows through walled pastures with gates and barns. The beck is always impressive, a fine waterfall being succeeded by a deep ravine into which there are dramatic peeps over the wall on its rim.'

The streams and becks here eventually gather into one of the great valleys of North Yorkshire. Swaledale and its river will accompany you on your walk for the next 30 miles (48.2 kilometres) or so to Richmond and beyond. This was Wainwright's favourite Yorkshire dale, somewhere that simply had to become part of his great trek across the country. AW describes Swaledale as simply 'delightful'.

Just in case I needed any convincing, on my arrival I was met with a spot of evening sunlight, not a bad first taste of life on the other side of the Pennines. Now at this point you've

An aerial view of the tiny village of Keld which marks the halfway point in the journey

got two choices, you can take the easy route, that's the road into Keld, or you can take the slightly tougher but more scenic route above the River Swale. As you can imagine AW recommends that you take the tougher route. Luckily, I'm a sucker for a good-looking view.

The final mile along the high path is, of course, well worth it, taking you above the cliffs and scars at the side of the tight valley to reveal a view down the first few miles of Swaledale to Keld. It might well be a tiny little outpost, truly tucked out of the way but this 'cluster of stone buildings…tidily yet haphazardly arranged' will no doubt be a very welcome sight. It's one of those special little spots were time seems almost frozen, a spot I'm not sure I would have had reason to visit were it not for the Coast to Coast walk. As AW noted: 'Little has changed here for generations past and proud dates and names of proud men adorn the doorways and walls and even the chapel belfry.' So, whilst Keld doesn't drip with amenities, its location more than compensates. AW wrote: 'The joy of Keld is the Swale. A swift-flowing torrent sheltered by white cliffs of limestone fringed with trees and broken by falls and cataracts on its fast course from the desolate hills to the soft pastures of the valley. Always, at Keld, there is the music of the river.'

This segment of the walk is about crossing boundaries, from the Lakes of Cumbria into the Dales of Yorkshire. But it will also be about stages of achievement – first at Nine Standards, for bagging the second highest summit on the journey, but also right here. By the time you take your boots off in the village of Keld you will be halfway through your Coast to Coast walk.

KELD IS HALFWAY!

Tears and Triumphs

Highlights: The five wonderful chocolate bars I consumed to get me across the moors.

Lowpoint: The weather was so bad there were ten expletives caught on tape with me cursing the rain.

KELD TO RICHMOND

Julia's Overview

For me, this section reminded me of how wonderful, odd and sometimes unexpected the places are that I get to meet people and share brief moments of what I think of as sort of walkers' camaraderie.

Yes, we walk to explore, to be in wild places and far-flung spots. The pleasure sometimes comes from the sheer isolation, or the grand remoteness, when striding out to discover that horizon in the distance can be truly uplifting. AW certainly encouraged his readers to head off on their own, without distraction. But there was one particular moment on this leg where I shared a brief conversation with a fellow walker, which just seemed to capture the spirit of a Coast to Coast walk.

My eighty-three-year old companion had pulled up at the same bench in Reeth, the halfway point in this section, as keen as me to simply soak up the moment in this mini-metropolis. He was on his sixth journey along a Coast to Coast and still enjoying every step. I'd asked him whether he planned more and he replied rather comically: 'I was told by a fortune teller in India that I would live till I was 108. I don't want to make a mockery of that man so I don't plan too far ahead. I don't even buy green bananas.' He went on to explain that on his travels he always asks his guides to remember two things. Should he suffer a heart attack en route they should roll him to one side so that people wouldn't be inconvenienced by stepping over him, and to remember that this old man died doing exactly what he wanted at the time. And with these words our bench side encounter was

A Coast to Coast marker post on the broad expanse of moorland above Swinner Gill, some 1,800 feet high
Pages 82-83: Swaledale flower meadows near Gunnerside

over, he simply turned around looked straight at me and said 'Now what more can you ask out of life'. And took his leave chuckling to himself as he went.

So, lessons do come in the least expected places and as for walking, well it's not just about putting one foot in front of the other…

The Castle Keep

Castle Walk

Richmond

THE WALK
SWALEDALE UNCOVERED
Keld to Richmond

DISTANCE: Keld to Reeth: 11 ¼ miles/18.1 kilometres
Reeth to Richmond: 10 ½ miles/16.8 kilometres
OS MAP: OL30 & 304

OVERVIEW

On leaving Keld you cross to the north side of the River Swale and follow it downstream. The route then branches up a beck and climbs steeply onto open moor tops. Today, this is favoured shooting land, but the scars and ruins of Victorian lead mining are everywhere. There's a slow descent back to the valley floor to the halfway point in Reeth, the key village at the heart of Swaledale. The walk through the lower valley continues along the river briefly, before branching south once again, across open farmland and into the quiet, untouched village of Marske. From here you walk underneath a line of cliffs that look down on the Swale as it winds its way to the end and rather exciting destination – the large Yorkshire town of Richmond.

The Walk

The countryside traversed is beautiful almost everywhere, yet extremely varied in character with mountains and hills, valleys and rivers, heather moors and sea cliffs combining in a pageant of colourful scenery.'
A. Wainwright

An aerial view of Swaledale, one of the great valleys of the Yorkshire Dales

You are now half way through your Coast to Coast walk. You've covered 95 miles (152.8 kilometres) from St Bees on the Irish Sea and you have another 95 miles (152.8 kilometres) to go before reaching Robin Hood's Bay. But for now it is all about Swaledale, one of the great valleys of the Yorkshire Dales. This is not the best known of Yorkshire's dales. but it was Wainwright's favourite and this section of my Coast to Coast adventure offers a complete Swaledale exploration.

Before I could leave Keld for the next section of the walk however, there was one lady I had to meet. Overlooking the village is a farm once owned by something of a Keld celebrity. Not only did Doreen Whitehead run a B&B for over twenty-four years, welcoming walkers from across the world, but in 1986 she was the first person to assemble a B&B guide, an accommodation bible no less, for walkers tackling AW's route, winning her the plaudit of 'Queen of the Coast to Coast.'

Swaledale

A view of Keld, the halfway point on the Coast to Coast route
AW wrote of Keld: '.. a sundial records the hours but time is measured in centuries at Keld.'

Much like its creator, this little guide is something of an institution. Although the use of internet research has caused sales of the guide to fall from up to 5,000 copies a year, to around 1,000 it is still very much available. In its early years Alfred Wainwright himself was so impressed with its recommendations he chose to drop in on Doreen midway through his own Coast to Coast walk. 'What a great man he was. I gave him a hug, told him that I loved him. He said 'well, that's you and Betty then…everyone else thinks I'm a miserable so-and-so. Walkers have such an impact on Keld my husband used to say we had mines for a hundred years, then farming and now it's walking. It's had a huge influence on the economy. Keld is the cross-point between the Coast to Coast and the Pennine Way. Lead mining has been dead for a century. Sheep farming has diminished dramatically. Tourism is everything and in Keld, the visitors are nearly all walkers.'

Julia at Keld Waterfalls

Doreen embodies everything that is so charming about Keld, it's a place that welcomes walkers from all over the world, yet retains the closest of communities and has a real sense of some surprising history.

Aside from an infamous landlady, Keld's other attractions include its well-known waterfalls. In this youthful stage of the Swale Valley countless tributaries tumble down the hillside to swell the waters of the river. At this stage you can also claim to be walking along two great routes, the Pennine Way and the Coast to Coast. One cuts across the country, the other goes up and down the country. The Pennine Way was actually one of the inspirations for AW's Coast to Coast. He thought he could come up with something more interesting and diverse. Swaledale sits at the very heart of the Coast to Coast walk. For most people, it's a two-day walk from Keld right the way down the valley to the major town of Richmond.

A view of the picturesque River Swale

And for once, Wainwright presents a very comfortable two day's walk, 22 miles (35.4 kilometres), so there's no need to rush...

Wainwright was clearly fascinated with Swaledale. He was understandably enchanted by the valley but it was the lead-mining industry that really piqued his interest. He wrote pages and pages about it. So at this point in the walk you have a choice, you can either walk 'along the lovely banks of the Swale, the first three miles to Muker especially being very beautiful.' Or you can saunter through the industrial landscape. AW certainly wrote favourably about it, suggesting 'the high-level route recommended in the following pages is of infinitely greater interest in addition to providing an excellent moorland walk made easy by use of miner's tracks.' So the choice is yours, the high road or the low road?

For me it was the higher option because I'm not one to ignore a recommendation from AW. Unlikely as it may seem these quiet hills high above the River Swale once rumbled with the noise of a massive local industry, which remains one of the biggest influences on this next section of the walk.

An aerial view of the ruins of Crackpot Hall, which was once at the centre of the lead mining industry in this area

At Crackpot Hall you can still see the ruins of this 'once handsome farmhouse (with a lovely view downriver to Muker)', that was once at the heart of the lead mining activity of this area. It's worth stopping for a moment to compare what stands today with AW's sketch of 1972. When I visited there was very little left, strangely most of the buildings to the left side had disappeared but it looked as if someone had popped a new roof on, odd, yet strangely in keeping with

the wonderfully eccentric name of the place. But the view from here is truly fantastic taking in a lovely curve of the River Swale. But from this point you say a temporary goodbye to the river. For those pursuing Wainwright's route of choice it's time to get amongst the hills.

Some 500 feet (152.4 metres) above its meeting with the River Swale, Swinner Gill Beck races off the hillside providing an obvious, if steep route, up onto the higher ground. I think it's safe to say that this path is probably more demanding than the one that follows the river. This section of the walk certainly allows you to get a feel for some of the industry AW was so intrigued by. He wrote: 'The sites of several abandoned lead mines are visited on the way, and although they are now ruinous, enough remains to enable the imaginative visitor to reconstruct the scene as it used to be when thousands of men toiled here.'

The reward for scrambling up the gill is a broad expanse of flat moorland plateau, around 1,800 feet (548.6 metres) high. This is classic terrain for grouse shooting and an idyllic, easy stroll if you're lucky to be here when the wind isn't blowing. No matter what the conditions though, the 4x4s, which plough a track here carrying gamekeepers and their clients, mean there's a very clear route to follow.

Gunnerside Gill

At this point in my walk I headed into what was once true mining country via Gunnerside Gill. The climb down is awkward, but dramatic, taking you on a walk through a manmade gorge known as a 'hush', a messed up world of mining destruction and the biggest sign yet of the impact one industry had on this area. As AW commented: 'The path along the east bank of Gunnerside Beck arrives suddenly at a remarkable area of devastation, a succession of hushes having gouged out much of the fellside ahead...nothing less like a Yorkshire Moor can be imagined.'

These manmade valleys were created by artificially damming water above and then letting it run downhill to wash away the top soil, sort of flushing out the hillside. AW described how this process would be done with such force 'as to strip the vegetation and scour the ground with the object of revealing any mineral content in the subsoil that might indicate the presence of a vein.' It was certainly a laborious task for these nineteenth-century prospectors who came here ('Today a bulldozer would be used', wrote AW).

The origins of this approach however, go as far back as ancient times and mining for lead is thought to have been carried out here by the Romans. But in Gunnerside Gill today, the evidence nearly all relates to two neighbouring mines Blakethwaite and Bunton. You can see numerous spoil heaps and entrances to levels dotted about all over the place. Where the Blakethwaite mine once rumbled with activity the remains of the smelting house and the peat store can be found.

Mining has clearly had a huge impact on this area. Starting in the Medieval period it continued right through to 1900. The 1821 census shows the key mining area had a population of over 8,000. By 1900 that same population had dropped dramatically to 3,000, lost to the coalfields of Durham, the

An aerial view overlooking the high-level route to Reeth, which AW describes as being '...of infinitely greater interest.'

cotton mills of Lancashire and even the more economic lead mines of Spain and America. Today Swaledale provides a very picturesque setting but it would have been such a different scene 200 years ago. This whole area would have been a hive of activity.

You have to wonder if the hills above Swaledale will ever recover from man's determination to plunder their lead. The view on the next hilltop is a stark reminder of some of that impact. AW noted: '...not a blade of grass nor a sprig of heather is seen, the natural moorland having been transformed into an arid desert of stone.'

This bit of the route doesn't take you through what you might necessarily consider beautiful landscape but it is still strangely captivating, perhaps because the desolation is in such contrast to the life and activity that once prospered here. During my walk it seemed strangely fitting that the weather began to deteriorate as I headed towards the stark

Julia above Swaledale

remains of one last industrial spot, the Old Gang Mines.

This was once an impressive operation and the largest lead producer in the area. The cloister-like ore stores are still just about discernible, standing uphill from the smelting mill itself. In 1840, this building produced 2,500 tonnes of lead. In 1910, it produced just 3. Today, it's hard to imagine that this site was in full working order less than a century ago. Lead still exists in these hills, but the best and the most accessible is gone and the skilled mining population that once filled the valley below has been lost forever. Today this is a landmark of a different kind. Here, you've chalked up the first 100 miles (160.9 kilometres) of your cross-country trek.

AW goes on to suggest that weary walkers today may benefit from some of the leftover residue of that development. 'Whether or not one approves of the ravaging of natural scenery on so vast a scale, the access roadway for vehicles leading down to the valley ahead is a great boom for foot

Looking towards Reeth, a popular halfway point on this section

travellers, who can make rapid progress along it and are spared the slow and wearying trudge over rough ground.' This is also the point where on a good day you might catch your first glimpse of the Cleveland Hills in the far distance, an early sign that you are starting to close in on your ultimate destination.

But for the immediate route the next key landmark comes in the shape of a classic Yorkshire Dales village. It might well be small but there's no doubting the significance of Reeth, the capital of Upper Swaledale. With schools, buses, pubs, hotels and even a museum, this is a place for locals and visitors. The enormous village green is the perfect spot to see Swaledale life pan out in front of you. For Coast to Coasters, Reeth is also the ideal place to break your journey down Swaledale. Ahead lies the simple trek to Richmond and the end of this great valley. When AW retraced his steps along the Coast to Coast route he spoke favourably of Reeth describing it as a'little civilised oasis' after the 'desolation of the leads mines.'

If my experience is anything to go by you may well find yourself bumping into other fellow walkers in such a cosy community. It's pretty easy to spot those other Wainwright wanderers across a bar. So, after a night's rest and a good deal of Coast to Coast nattering it's on to the very sizeable goal of Richmond.

AW describes this next part of the route favourably, so there's plenty to look forward to. He wrote: 'This section is short and easily accomplished, but is so abundantly endowed with variety and beauty and interest that it would be unforgivable to rush it in half a day.' Whilst Wainwright certainly liked his mines it has generally meant a bit more scrambling and tougher inclines. So for this next bit it's certainly nice to amble along the riverbank.

This will also be your first close encounter with the River Swale since leaving Keld, a reunion, which certainly enthused AW who wrote: 'the scenery throughout this section is of high quality, with the Swale the dominant feature and lovely everywhere.' To me it also started to look broader here and a good deal more sedate. But there's a familiar rusty tint, a reminder that this water has come straight from the peat bogs of the Pennines.

The Swale at Richmond

True to form, Wainwright soon manages to find some higher ground in need of exploring, taking his followers on another adventure away from the river, across the rolling farmland of the lower Swale towards the village of Marske.

AW pays compliment to its position: 'Marske lies snugly sequestered amongst fine trees in a side valley of Swaledale, a glacial fold in the hills, fringed by limestone cliffs with wild heathery moors beyond. The charm of the place is its natural scenery.' But I do think you can feel a bit sorry for Marske, it sort of gets overlooked. At this stage of the Coast to Coast most people are hell bent on getting to Richmond, which is the only significant town on the entire walk.

In such a long distance walk it's probably no surprise to be getting just a little bit excited about the prospect of a town and all the facilities and amenities it will bring. You can do some washing, stock up on plasters at the chemist, chocolate supplies, you can even go to the theatre should you need to top up on some culture. You may well be feeling the bright lights of town life calling.

But it's worth putting these thoughts on hold for just a little while longer. The last 3 miles (4.8 kilometres) of this section provide a fantastic traverse walk along the sidewall of lower Swaledale. This high-level path offers one last lingering look down onto the Swale, before all walkers disappear into one of those rare things on the Coast to Coast, a wood. For me Whitcliffe Wood was a rather quiet, dark and very damp place on an autumn evening. But it would be a haven of bluebells and primroses in spring.

This portion of the Coast to Coast route offers a pretty satisfying tramp along the entire length of Swaledale. The river starts as a bubbling torrent in Keld and becomes something rather more gentle and meandering. This section provides an itinerary of varying interest with moorland, woodland, and some mining history too.

For now though, there's just one more sight to see.

Spotting the Norman keep of Richmond's castle is quite a contrast after all the wide-open countryside you've walked through. Setting your sights on this is also quite an unusual ambition for a Wainwright Walk... but nevertheless it will probably feel quite welcome at this stage in your march across England.

Tears and Triumphs

Highlights: A very plump scone, jam and cream in Reeth. Well deserved by that point I'd say.

Lowpoint: Soggy soggy socks.

RICHMOND TO BLAKEY RIDGE

Julia's Overview

Now, this chapter offers both highlight and humdrum. Unfortunately to get to the highlight you have to take on some of the 'interminable', in the shape of the Vale of Mowbray. Love it or loath it will lead you onwards to better things and what comes next is in such sharp contrast that somehow it seems all the sweeter and worth waiting for. So for me part one of this section delivered another lesson in the art of long-distance walking, where I learned that patience is certainly a virtue and taking the 'rough with the smooth' an essential.

Get through these flatlands and you'll discover the next best thing outside AW's beloved fells, which he heralds as the 'finest section of our marathon'. The Cleveland Hills and North York Moors may well be the runner-ups to AW's Lakeland but at this stage on the route I remember it felt like a new chapter. Here was a new kind of Wainwright territory, it had all the familiar hallmarks of AW's stomping grounds but it was unexplored and it seemed full of new possibilities. It was great to again have that feeling of new heights to gain and fresh panoramas that could unfold. I hadn't ever done any proper walking here so that in itself brought a new spring to my step. Exploring somewhere new reminded me again of one of the motivations behind AW's Coast to Coast Walk. He was always keen to emphasise that his guide was merely one offering, one possible route that would take you on this great cross country adventure. What he hoped it would inspire however was a spirit of adventure, that desire to poke your nose into new places and step out discovering a route for yourself.

Julia on the North Yorks Moors
Pages 102-103: The route over Live Moor

AW wrote: 'The point I want to emphasise is that the route herein described is in no sense an 'official route' such as the Pennine Way – it has not needed the approval of the Countryside Commission or indeed any other body nor have any permissions needed to be sought. It is a harmless and enjoyable walk across England, entirely (so far as I am aware) on existing rights of way or over ground where access is traditionally free to all.'

In other words – feel free to create your own adventure. And I do so like that thought. I'm not saying everyone has to walk across England to discover their sense of adventure but… it might just help.

The Wainstones:
the lower rocks

The Wainstones:
the upper rocks

THE WALK

MILES & MOORS: Richmond to Blakey Ridge

DISTANCE: 45 miles/72.4 kilometres
OS MAP: 304 & OL26

OVERVIEW

From Richmond the route enters the notorious Vale of Mowbray, 15 miles (24.1 kilometres) that's as flat as a pancake. Love it or hate it, every walker seems to have an opinion on it. Crossing the busy A19 you reach the peaceful Mount Grace Priory at the foot of the Cleveland Hills where there's the challenge of an undulating escarpment along the North York Moors. The rewards are many, including the favourite rocky outcrop known as the Wainstones. These broad open heathlands are also the terrain of thousands of grouse and the gamekeepers that look after them. Today the route of the old Rosedale branch line takes you all the way to the end target, Blakey Ridge and the most remote of overnight spots, the Lion Inn.

The Walk

'The walk detailed in this book is my own preference, but some walkers may choose to vary it in places, either to make additional detours or to short-cut corners, or even follow their own course over lengthy distances. Such personal initiatives are to be encouraged – if they do not involve trespass. The way you go and the time it takes matters not. The essence of the walk is the crossing of England, from one coast to the other, on foot.'
A. Wainwright

An aerial view over the town of Richmond nestled around its Norman castle

By the time you reach Richmond you will have already crossed the Lake District, the Pennines and followed the River Swale for 23 miles (37 kilometres). So I think it's fair to say you deserve just a few hours off for a snoop round this lovely historic town. Richmond is after all, by far the most significant town on the route and it would also appear that even the solitary Wainwright loved this place describing it as 'a town unlike others' and a place 'rich in relics of the past, steeped in a long history that still lingers in the ramifications of its castle and the narrow alleys and quaint buildings that huddle in the shelter of the massive Norman keep.' AW clearly felt that its charms and history warranted a trip into civilization. After everything you've now walked through Richmond is quite simply 'too good to be by-passed', in fact it could be very easy to get waylaid here because the next portion of the walk is pretty challenging. What you have to face next is the flat Vale of Mowbray, followed by the rugged North York Moors and that's a lot of ground to cover.

More than any other, this section is a walk of contrasts. It cuts through a huge part of north Yorkshire, England's biggest county. An initially long trudge across flat farming land will however be rewarded by the open wilderness of the North York Moors. This chapter covers the next 45 miles (72.4 kilometres) of the Coast to Coast walk, making it the longest section I cover in this book. For most walkers this would however, be broken down into at least three days hard slog.

Now, before you get well and truly stuck into the route there is one final distraction in Richmond, which you just have to see. The town's impressive waterfalls stand directly

Richmond's impressive waterfalls stand directly beneath the great walls of its Norman castle

beneath the great walls of the Norman castle. Having never come under attack the castle remains very much as it was eight hundred years ago and today proudly watches over a bustling town centre. Most visitors to the town come to this spot, to see one of England's fastest flowing rivers, but only Coast to Coasters can say they've followed the Swale all the way here.

Heading away from Richmond you follow the river downstream as it flows on its own journey towards the coast. The Swale makes for a good walking companion and by this point you have already been through quite a bit together. But this rather blissful easiness is shattered by Britain's longest road, the thundering A1, which rather like the M6 some 60 miles ago, now carves up the Coast to Coast walk again in a fairly unpleasant manner. But it's an obstacle you don't have to face head on. Sadly, this also means you will shortly be saying your final goodbye to the river. The last echo of the Swale is in name only as you reach the pretty village of Bolton-on-Swale.

At this point you might like a brief detour. Thanks to

Julia in Richmond

Wainwright, not many people could now pass through without stopping at St Mary's Churchyard to investigate a rather curious local story, a legend that an elderly AW was keen to show Eric Robson when they were filming for the BBC. The archive footage shows AW taking Eric to find the stone obelisk and then reading the inscription: 'erected by contribution in the year 1743 to the memory of Henry Jenkins.' The unusual part is that Mr Jenkins is supposed to have died aged 169.

Now it does seem rather unlikely doesn't it, this would mean that local fisherman and occasional roof-thatcher Henry Jenkins would have witnessed Henry VIII, Shakespeare and the Great Fire of London. It seems clear that Henry Jenkins died in 1670, but quite when he was born is more questionable, occurring some time before parish records began. But this unconfirmed, record-breakingly old man clearly raised a wry smile from Wainwright.

The Jenkins Memorial,

But it is a brief distraction from '*that*' section.

An aerial view over the flatlands of the Vale of Mowbray

During my Coast to Coast walk it was the one part of the route I wasn't sure I was entirely looking forward to, But you can avoid it no longer and lingering in graveyards can only go on for so long. The Vale of Mowbray now awaits and even AW seemed rather less enthused by the road ahead. He wrote of this next section: 'You have heard of Yorkshire's broad acres, here they are in person, interminable, neatly patterned by clipped thorn hedges or wooden fences, but never, never a stone wall: a foreign land indeed.'

This is the longest stretch of road-walking on the whole Coast to Coast route. The views really are of the road ahead and the fields alongside and then miles and miles of country lanes, which seem to go on and on. It's a far cry indeed from the drama of AW's cherished Lakeland, which he acknowledges. 'To walkers whose liking is for high places and rough terrain, this will seem the dullest part of the whole walk; those who believe the earth is flat will be mightily encouraged on this section.' You only need to take a peek at this section of AW's guide and his perspiring self-portrait sketch, to see that even the great man found this bit heavy going.

The one oasis right in the middle of the Vale is the village of Danby Wiske, an essential stop off for Coast to Coasters, most of whom head straight to the village pub. Annoyingly for me though I arrived much too early in the day and so found the door firmly closed. But at least my frustration was strangely in keeping because in the Coast to Coast guide, Wainwright notes with disdain that after the long tarmac trek from Richmond, all he could get from Danby Wiske was a bag of crisps. Well at least he got that much. (I should add that I'm reliably informed the Swan Inn does cook up some lovely hearty fayre, you just need to plan lunch for some time after noon during the months of April to October).

Whilst this won't necessarily feel like the most inspirational section of the walk it will at least allow you to tick off some miles in a perfunctory sort of fashion. I found that it also allowed a bit of anticipation to grow, which meant I was really looking forward to seeing the North York Moors. In fact, I was looking forward to seeing anything!

Sheep were a regular feature on my Coast to Coast walk but in this flattest of farming territory there's larger livestock too, with herds of cattle dotting the fields, queuing up for attention. Across this open farmland you will see the next challenge rearing upwards, in the shape of the Cleveland Hill. This means you are now headed for the walk's third National Park, the North York Moors. This upland view also means the crossing of the Vale of Mowbray is almost at an end. But the final sting in the tail is another one of those major roads. Unlike the M6 and A1 there's no way around it. You need all your concentration here because frankly it's terrifying. To be fair to my walk's creator, the traffic was presumably less

The peaceful Mount Grace Priory. AW wrote that it is 'one of the best surviving examples of the few Carthusian foundations in this country.'
Right: Julia at Mount Grace Priory

threatening in 1972. Once you make it across though it's time for a minor celebration. You have now completed two thirds of the Coast to Coast.

The nearby village of Ingleby Cross is a popular overnight stop for most walkers at this stage. So, after a night's rest you will probably be keen to get stuck into the undoubted highlight of this section, the northern shoulder of the North York Moors, those Cleveland Hills. AW was clearly greatly enthused by the area: 'This is the finest section of our marathon (outside Lakeland) – a splendid high-level traverse along the escarpment of the Cleveland Hills: beautiful country with far reaching views.'

The gateway to these impressive heights is a surprising

Coast to Coast treat. Nestled at the foot of the hills is Mount Grace Priory, one of the best surviving examples of a Carthusian foundation in the country. Here the monks lived a hermit like existence in total seclusion and silence and the arrangement of their quarters around a large walled cloister can still be seen. It's rare for Wainwright to direct you to a place of manmade and not natural, beauty but wandering around these fourteenth century ruins you can see why it was a favourite, a spot almost as reclusive as AW himself.

It's nice to relax in such tranquil surroundings but once you leave, hard work beckons and it's a very welcome return to true Wainwright upland walking. Just a quarter of a mile away are the overgrown remains of the quarry where the stone was found to build the priory. It's a well-hidden landmark that points the way to the third great wilderness of the Coast to Coast walk.

Heading eastwards into the heather strewn slopes of the North York Moors you then follow the clear path running

An aerial view of the approach to the rocky outcrop known as the Wainstones

along the escarpment, the beginning of the final stage of the walk. The fine landscape stretches out ahead with miles of stunning heather covering a great range of moortops, each with their own individual name. It's a landscape that rises and falls 500 feet (152.4 metres) with alarming regularity. The top of Carlton Moor is amongst the flattest. As AW mentions, it is 'eerily lunar' and deserted 'the heather having been stripped off and the surface bulldozed and levelled to make runways for a gliding club whose buildings can be seen ahead.' AW describes gliding as both a 'thrilling' and 'graceful' exercise but you can't ignore the impact of this sport on the scenery. He wrote: '…not even the most ardent enthusiast will claim that the landscape has been improved by its conversion to runways and some may even agree that a large tract of natural scenery has been despoiled. Well, there can be no comment from an 'off-comer' except to say that if such an operation was to be planned for the top of Helvellyn all hell would be let loose.'

The Carlton Moor Gliding Club has sat 1,300 feet (396

The Wainstones which AW described as a 'cluster of fanged and pinnacled rocks.'

metres) up since the early 1960s but you may notice in this day and age the sport has a new competitor. Where gliders once filled the skies high above the moors, you're now much more likely to see paragliders dotting the sky. You don't need an expensive aircraft, you don't need any winches, you just need a patch of open grassland and a slope you can chuck yourself off, and I'd say a lot of nerve. For those with less nerve, there's also a much noisier option… paramotoring. To me this rather looks like you take the same parachute and strap a big fan to your back. It's certainly allows you to motor through the skies but perhaps a little more intrusively, I'm not entirely sure Wainwright would have approved.

These distractions are all well and good but there's walking to be done. A good next goal is the massive bulk of Cringle End, the highest spot yet on the Cleveland Hills and with its steep edge, it's the most impressive. From up here you can look back on Carlton and Live Moor and the Vale of Mowbray stretching all the way back to Richmond and then forwards to the route ahead and the peaks you have

Boundary stone and Ordnance column, summit of Carlton Moor

yet to conquer. Another three moortops lie waiting on the route ahead, whilst far to the north is the 'mini-Matterhorn' looking peak named Roseberry Topping. The views here are amongst the broadest on the Coast to Coast walk, the massive petrochemical works at Teesside being one of the few blots.

Apart from that, this stretch of the walk is classic Wainwright, more rugged than the Lake District, less pretty than the Yorkshire Dales but with the unmistakable variety and adventure you'd expect from a Wainwright walk. The route now leads to the best known spot on the Cleveland Hills, the Wainstones, 'a cluster of fanged and pinnacled rocks.' AW advises: 'This is an enjoyable section, a change from heather, and there is no difficulty in scrambling between the buttresses to the easy ground above. You will like the Wainstones.'

By this point you may feel that you have been on an exhausting roller coaster of moors, but each summit seems to keep you going and is more impressive than the last. Wainwright is emphatically positive about the Cleveland Hills and I don't think he was over stating it either. An easy and

After the Wainstones have been negotiated an easy and majestic stroll across the top of the moors follows

majestic stroll across the top of the moors follows and it leads to Round Hill, the very highest point on the Cleveland Hills. It's a quiet place, free from all the attention of the Wainstones and with a quite different quality and stillness.

The hard work may have been done but there's still a stretch to go before the final target of Blakey Ridge. But Wainwright clearly loved this particular spot for one very good reason. As you make your final approach you get to follow the beautifully flat path left behind from the Rosedale Ironstone Railway.

Up on the moors, some 1,200 feet (365.7 metres) high seemed one of the most unlikely places I've ever found a disused railway line. This Victorian engineering feat avoids the need for any bridges or tunnels by winding its way in great loops around the heads of valleys, all the time sticking solidly to the same contour. But its existence certainly helps

The Lion Inn – undoubtedly the most isolated overnight spot on the Coast to Coast

with the route today, a fact AW all too wisely noted: 'Fast walking continues along the railway track and speeds will now have accelerated to 5mph.'

From the railway the view to the south is of the tranquil valley of Farndale, a beautiful sight at the end of the day, although AW suggests you 'resist' its attractions as it 'specialises in daffodils, not beds and surge on happily.' It's clear Wainwright found the old track made for happy walking. He enthused: 'We're enjoying this: it's like playing at trains again. Better than that, it's like being a train yourself.'

But you still have to 'choo choo' your way to the final goal of Blakey Ridge where you will find, without doubt the most isolated, overnight spot on the whole Coast to Coast walk. As you reach a curve in the last railway cutting you will finally spot The Lion Inn, which AW described as 'a good moment'. This solitary building is the first 'habitation since Huthwaite, 16 miles back' and 'the most obvious halting-place on the whole route.'

It's now been 45 miles (72.4 kilometres) since Richmond,

The Lion Inn, Blakey

Dating from 1553, the Lion is an isolated moorland inn. Situated amongst decayed relics of industry, it once catered for ironworkers and coalminers but today it serves walkers and motorists (and looks somewhat different from this drawing).

you've said goodbye to the River Swale, made it through the Vale of Mowbray and conquered the Cleveland Hills. You will probably now only have around two full walking days to go, so you might just be starting to feel you are on the home straight.

Tears and Triumphs

Highlights: Fish and chips with lashings of vinegar – I take my lead from AW.

Lowpoint: Back to same old sarnies for lunch…not a pie in sight for miles.

BLAKEY RIDG
ROBIN HOOD'S BA

Julia's Overview

Reaching this stage was of course momentous. This was the home straight, the end was in sight and what at times had seemed like the mythical promised land in the distance, was just a few miles away. Like any walker the final sections of a long-distance route can inspire a whole mixture of feelings. I genuinely started to feel that buzz of the finishing line, the heady excitement of the end goal (as well as a rather compelling desire for a bag of chips with lashings of vinegar. I'm sure it was the prospect of all that sea air). I also had a train to catch to start another job in Scotland.

But alongside that flush of anticipation there was something else, the strange and inevitable fact that all of this was also about to end. A long-distance walk really gets under your skin. You and 'it' are, after all, with each other day after day. So the prospect of finally parting company seemed to stir a strange mixture of elation and a mellow sort of sadness. So, for others approaching this stage with this rather odd cocktail of feelings may I medicate with some of AW's wise words: 'One should always have a definite objective, in a walk as in life – it is so much more satisfying to reach a target by personal effort than to wander aimlessly. An objective is an ambition, and life without ambition is...well, aimless wandering.'

A Coast to Coast is one walk, there's also the matter of Wainwright's 214 Lakeland fells to tackle as well as forty odd other books to peruse and plan from. So, if you are feeling a little 'aimless' there is plenty of inspiration out there – but don't forget to create your own adventures.

Julia at Robin Hood's Bay
Pages 122-123: The first glimpse of Robin Hood's Bay

Robin Hood's Bay

THE WALK

THE END OF THE ROAD

Blakey Ridge to Robin Hood's Bay

DISTANCE: 29 miles/46.6 kilometres
OS MAP: OL 26 & 27

OVERVIEW

Leaving The Lion Inn you spend the first 7 miles (11.2 kilometres) striding out across the tops of the moors. The route rounds the head of Great Fryup Dale, with a view onto green fields from the lofty path. The long finger of Glaisdale Rigg, takes you down slowly into the Eskdale Valley and through the three villages of Glaisdale, Egton Bridge and lastly, Grosmont, home of the North York Moors steam railway. The climb out of Eskdale provides a true landmark as it's here that you will gain your first view of the North Sea. It quickly disappears though, as you head down into the tranquil Little Beck Valley. From here, it's all about reaching the end of this great adventure, finally arriving on the cliffs, south of Whitby. The Coast to Coast walk ends with a lap of honour with 2 miles (3.2 kilometres) of cliff top strolling, that lead to the coastal village, which has been your ambition for so long... Robin Hood's Bay.

The Walk

"The objective in this book is Robin Hood's Bay, on the Yorkshire coast: doubly satisfying because it is not only an attractive place to finish a walk but also very definitive: here land ends and sea begins. You can't walk on water, and Robin Hood's Bay is a definite full stop, a terminus absolute.

A. Wainwright

An aerial view of the last section of the walk across fields to the coast

I started this section on what felt like the top of the North York Moors after an overnight stay at The Lion Inn. There's been a farmhouse here since the sixteenth century, but it's only since the Coast to Coast walk was conceived that people started walking 162 miles (260.7 kilometres just to get here. This inn, here at Blakey Ridge, is perhaps the most obvious overnight spot on the entire Coast to Coast walk. From this lofty position, it's downhill as you begin the final stretch of this great walk, North Sea here you come.

(I do have one cautionary note and that's book early. Exhausted Coast to Coast walkers would be unwise to arrive here without a reservation as it's a fair old way to the next nearest bed. It's well worth staying too, once inside, you'll find an inn resounding with tales of adventures acquired on the route from the Irish Sea, just what you need to fuel your last gasp of enthusiasm for the final section).

So, once that next day arrives if you are anything like me it will start to slowly dawn that this is it, the beginning of the end. But there's not really the time to reminisce just yet, you've still plenty of moorland to cover, a glut of Yorkshire villages and a dramatic coastline, if the legs can hold up. Try and keep them going because at this stage you are so close to being able to claim your prize of having walked from one side of England to the other and that is surely something worth keeping going for. AW suggests walkers may even 'consider this section the best of all, quite apart from the satisfaction of accomplishing a mission.' His enthusiasm for the route ahead may certainly lift any tiring spirits. He wrote encouragingly: 'You will really enjoy this last section to the Bay, whatever the conditions of

your blisters, so much so that you will regret leaving behind each of its many attractive features.'

By now you are already deep into the third National Park but from The Lion Inn, there's just 27 miles (43.4 kilometres) separating you from the coastline. The final moors, valleys and woods await, before a triumphant arrival along the cliffs to your ultimate destination. But before that there are still plenty of mini landmarks to tick off, not least those of Rosedale Head, which include a 'Fat Betty,' which Wainwright even made a little sketch of. This part of the moors is littered with an assortment of stone monuments and obelisks. Most have a mythical story attached to them and have long been a landmark for travellers and wayfarers plotting their path across these exposed lands. It is traditional to leave a food offering for the next walker. When I visited someone had left a hard-boiled sweet, so I scoffed that and replaced it with a hearty muesli bar.

An aerial view over Great Fryup Dale

From here a branch right leads to a rather solitary building known as Trough House, an old shooting hut, which Wainwright described as 'such an excellent refuge that one almost wishes it could rain cats and dogs so that advantage could be taken of its shelter.'

You probably won't want to linger but the setting is nevertheless majestic and worth soaking up. A few hundred yards away is the head of the bizarrely named Great Fryup Dale. You might well ask what a 'fryup' has to do with the goddess of beauty. Well, the valley in front of you isn't actually named after eggs and bacon, but rather the Norse goddess of beauty, Freya. The Old English word for a remote valley was 'hop', making this valley, Freya's Hop which over the course of centuries has evolved into the rather more amusing – 'Fry up'.

When you look at the map, you can make out the shapes of the

moors and the valleys. Fryup Dale is surrounded by high fingers of land on either side, one of which is Glaisdale Rigg, which brings the last bit of upland before you head down to the villages below.

The approach to the first village is a bit like a scene from a road movie, there's a 3 mile (4.8 kilometres) long track that slowly descends along Glaisdale Rigg making for a rather open and windswept goodbye to the last stretch of consistent high ground on the Coast to Coast walk.

This leads you all the way to Glaisdale the first real outpost of humanity since Ingleby Cross and that was before the moors about 30 miles (48.2 kilometres) back. In Glaisdale, humanity is of a fairly unobtrusive kind though, so it won't be too much of a shock to the system. But there's one particularly peaceful landmark, easily the most photographed and sketched structure in town that's well worth stopping off for. In the seventeenth century a local lad desperate to find an easier way to woo his lover on the other side of the river built Beggar's Bridge. Sadly, the Coast to Coast route doesn't

Julia at the North York Moors Railway

actually cross it, but that's no reason not to go and try it out.

A short walk through dense woodland is all it takes to reach the next village in Eskdale, Egton Bridge. Here, there really is a chance to cross the River Esk, before path, river and railway line all follow the valley floor for two miles to the third and largest village of Grosmont.

Grosmont is a lot less sleepy than its neighbouring villages. It's got shops, and pubs and it's even got its own railway, The North York Moors Railway. This was here long before Wainwright invented, thought, or even dreamt of the Coast to Coast route.

Grosmont Station dates back to the 1830s but today it's an attraction that remains permanently in the 1950s. For some 300,000 visitors each year, very little has in fact changed since

An aerial view, which shows the climb out of the Eskdale Valley where you will be rewarded with your first views of the North Sea

steam enthusiast Alfred Wainwright first arrived here on his passage across the country in 1989.

The original line, which was a branch line from Whitby to Pickering was axed in 1965 during a swathe of dramatic cuts undertaken by the notorious Dr Beeching. But two years later a determined band of railway enthusiasts got together and acquired what remained of the old track that hadn't been taken up. This amounted to a stretch of 18 miles (28.9 kilometres) across the moors to Pickering and they preserved everything, signals and all. This means today's visitors can still take a very pleasant cross-country steam journey. The star of the show when I was there was the Sir Nigel Gresley, a beautifully styled A4 class locomotive that once pulled express services at over 100mph; a truly mighty beast indeed.

Train buffs may well find it a little harder to drag themselves away but leaving the railway means it's also time to leave the Eskdale Valley. From here, there's just 16 miles (25.7 kilometres) to reach the end of this great adventure. So with half your mind already on that east coast, I've no doubt the climb out of Grosmont takes most Coast to Coasters somewhat by surprise. You might well have the sound of steam engines ringing in your ears but this is a hill and a half. The view is at least some compensation. The whole of Eskdale is laid out on a plate with views back over Grosmont, the woods, Glaisdale and even the moors beyond. But this is the last steep climb of the walk and then, hopefully, all being well, a sight will be revealed that every Coast to Coaster waits patiently for.

AW wrote: 'The moment of arrival at Flat Howe is historic, for a view is here revealed that has been anticipated eagerly. From this ancient burial mound can be seen ahead, indubitably, the Promised Land (and Sea).'

So, as you finally break out onto this last summit point of the route you should be able to spot it, finally the North Sea. There's also Whitby Abbey, and if you cast your eyes round to the right, those craggy silhouettes in the grey mist are the cliffs around Robin Hood's Bay. You can surely smell the end and a sea breeze?

As finishing straights go this is certainly a long one but perhaps that's only fitting after days and days of eating up nearly 200 miles (321.8 kilometres). There's still time for Wainwright to throw in a few surprises, the first involving a 900-foot (274.3-metre) descent into the almost unimaginable valley of Little Beck.

According to the great man this is 'a miniature arcadia embowered with trees, a glimpse of heaven for nerve-frayed town dwellers'. It's also a welcome change from the bleakness of the moors. But there is something slightly unreal

One final clifftop stroll leads to Robin Hood's Bay

about Little Beck, it's undeniably beautiful, but it seems so unconnected from the outside world. It feels like you have wandered into a nursery rhyme.

At this stage in my walk it was rather a nice spot to pause for a moment's reflection on this grand adventure and it was also where I was able to meet up with an old Wainwright acquaintance. Mark Richards is a writer and broadcaster who I'd met on a number of my Lakeland walks, but he was also a friend and walking partner of AW and he'd had the enviable good fortune to join Wainwright as he finalised his Coast to Coast route. 'Wainwright was fundamental to me all those years ago back in the 1970s. I had the golden opportunity of actually getting to know him. I visited him and really engaged with his whole world, his outdoor world and his creative world and it influenced me tremendously. He had such a unique style, it came from another age making his books so distinctive. They embodied his personality in such a way I was riveted by them.

He didn't know the North York Moors very well at all so he

A welcome sight for weary Coast to Coast walkers who reach Robin Hood's Bay; The End

came over this side and he actually walked from Richmond across the Vale of Mowbray with its notorious road sections and then across the escarpment to Robin Hood's Bay and once he knew that worked he backtracked to the Lake District and went to St Bees and worked his way through. He walked it backwards and forwards, it was disjointed in a certain respect but of course it meant he was in full command of it. He knew the Lake District section worked, he left the cream on the cake with the Westmorland Plateau where I joined him and then over Nine Standards Rigg and through Swaledale and his great moment was the arrival in Richmond.'

However long you linger in Little Beck it's no surprise that from here on in your thoughts turn entirely to the North Sea. For these last few miles you can forget your aches and pains and the blisters will no longer seem a distraction. It's best foot forward with a surge of new energy, across flat fields, straight to the village of Hawsker, which is absolutely, without doubt, the last settlement before Robin Hood's Bay.

It's no surprise that AW wanted to complete his great

Hawsker
(omitting the TV aerials but including the drainpipes)

adventure with a flourish and you will no doubt feel you haven't come this far not to end it properly. The main road to Robin Hood's Bay is signed from Hawsker but that would have been no way to round off the Coast to Coast. AW indeed warns it 'is a temptation to be resisted' encouraging instead a clifftop stroll. He wrote: 'the royal road to the Bay undoubtedly is the coast path…That's the way we'll go, so carry on down the lane and don't argue.'

Finally reaching the sea is quite a moment and for the next 3 or 4 miles you hug the edge of the cliffs which AW described as 'excellent scenery'. But the final prize is yet to come, you turn the corner at Ness Point and suddenly there it is, Robin Hood's Bay

Just like the very beginning of my walk, the end of the Coast to Coast walk shows off just what the British coastline has to offer. When I filmed my television series nearly three weeks had passed since we'd set out from St Bees. Since then, my hardy crew and I had been drenched and dried out too many times to number. I'd scaled the ranges of the Lakes, trampled the bogs of the Pennines and trudged the roads of the Vale of Mowbray, crossed the Cleveland Hills and the Moors. But there I was once again, 300 feet (91.4

An aerial view of Robin Hood's Bay, the final destination

metres) above crashing waves. Once you reach this point it becomes your walk of triumph, not expectation.

People are drawn here for all manner of reasons. Some try the Coast to Coast walk for the challenge itself. Others, for the exploration and discovery, or the friends and acquaintances they will meet and then there are those, who come back again and again, always learning something new about northern England and about themselves. In 1991 a guy called Mike Hartley even ran the Coast to Coast route in under forty hours, although of course speed was never an issue for Wainwright.

Who knows just how many thousands have completed this walk. But the adventure today, remains almost exactly as it did in 1973 when Wainwright first created it.

Wainwright saves the much-anticipated final view until the very last minute. I'm not surprised he chose to avoid the grand towns of Whitby and Scarborough and end his walk in the quirky, more personal setting of Robin Hood's Bay. St Bees Head and Robin Hood's Bay are names that are so firmly etched in your mind throughout this walk that actually finally arriving was genuinely exciting for me.

As you make your way through the twist of narrow streets I'm sure the vast majority of the crowds here are totally unaware of the personal achievement about to occur in front of them. AW's final instructions are clear. He wrote: 'Go forward and put your boot in the first salt-water puddle. By this ritual you will have completed a walk from one side of England to the other.'

As you finally let that seawater lap at your boots you can't help but soak in all that you've just achieved. The Coast to Coast is more than just a walk. It's an adventure, it's about the people you meet, the stories you hear and the histories that you pass through. And of course it's about getting your feet wet, (sometimes even daily).

Over the years, with the help of Alfred Wainwright, I've got to know his Lake District very well. This walk brought a new offering and some new destinations. These walking

Now you can rest on your laurels in the Bay Hotel with a pint, but (let there be no misunderstanding about this) you do so at your own expense. It's no use saying "charge it to Wainwright" as you could in days gone by at the Border Hotel, Kirk Yetholm. No, sonny, that game won't work here. Pay for your own. I'm skint.

landscapes, just like the Lakes are rich in texture and diversity and despite some awful weather along the way, had been just as welcoming. Nearly 200 miles (321.8 kilometres) is a hefty walk but this really is a momentous cross-country journey. Once again Wainwright proved himself to be the perfect company, every step of the way. So, on that note I'll leave you with some of AW's wisest words, which I think help seal this route as one of the truly great long distance walks:

'...when the North Sea comes into full view and you recall your last sighting of the Irish Sea you will be glad you didn't stay on in Patterdale. Lakeland is all very well but by resisting its lure you have seen so much new and interesting and lovely country that, on reflection, you wouldn't have missed for worlds. Come on now, admit it.'

Tears and Triumphs

Highlights: There's nothing quite like that first whiff of a sea breeze (and the prospect of another bag of chips).

Lowpoint: Realising Fryup Dale was not going to be serving up a sizzling bacon sarnie for elevenses...

INDEX

A
Angle Tarn 56
Angler's Crag 33
Angler's Hotel 32, 37

B
Betty (Wainwright) 90
Beggar's Bridge 132
Black Sail Youth Hostel 34
Blakethwaite Mine 95
Blakey Ridge 107, 120, 129
Bolton-on-Swale 110
Borrowdale 23, 36, 38, 45, 47, 48, 53
Buttermere 36

C
Carlton Moor 116, 117
Cleator 29
Cleveland Hills 98, 104, 113, 114, 117 – 121, 138
Coronation Day 52
Crackpot Hall 93
Cringle End 117
Crummock Water 36
Cumbria 23, 47, 58, 71, 76, 81

D
Danby Wiske 113
Dent 23, 29
Doreen Whithead (Queen of the Coast to Coast) 89 – 91

E
Easedale 45
Eastern Fells 50
Eden Valley 58, 67, 69, 71, 73, 74
Edmund Hillary 52
Egton Bridge 127, 133
Ennerdale 23, 31, 33, 36, 37
Ennerdale Bridge 30, 31, 36
Ennerdale Forest 33, 34
Ennerdale Water 23, 31 – 33, 39
Eric Robson 27, 48, 52, 71, 111
Eskdale Valley 127, 134, 135

F
Fairfield 45, 50
Fleetwith Pike 38

G
Glaisdale 127, 132, 135
Glaisdale Rigg 127, 132
Grasmere 45, 48, 49, 50, 52
Great Fryup Dale 127, 131
Great Gable 34, 35
Green Gable 34
Greenup Edge 45
Grisedale 45, 52
Grisedale Tarn 50, 51
Grosmont 127, 133, 135
Gunnerside Gill 94, 95

H
Haweswater 45, 57 – 59
Haystacks 23, 34
Helvellyn 45, 50, 53
Henry Jenkins 111
High Crag 34
High Street 56, 57
Honister Pass 23, 36
Honister (slate) 37, 38

I
Ingleby Cross 114
Irish Sea 20, 23 – 25, 30, 47, 89, 129
Isle of Man 29

K
Keld 67, 80, 81, 87, 89 – 91, 99, 101
Kendal 49
Kidsty Pike 45, 56, 57, 59, 61
Kirkby Stephen 67, 69 – 72
Kirk Fell 34

L
Lake District (National Park) 25, 30, 47, 59, 69, 109, 118, 137, 138, 140
Lakeland 26, 27, 29 – 32, 36, 38, 42, 45, 47, 49, 50, 53, 55 – 59, 61, 64, 74, 104, 112, 136, 141

Lake Windermere 71
Lion Inn 107, 120, 127, 129, 130
Little Beck Valley 127
Loft Beck 35

M
Mardale 57
Mark Richards 136
Mark Weir 37
Marske 87, 100
Moor Row 28
Mount Grace Priory 107, 115

N
Nannycatch 30
Nine Standards Rigg 67, 72 – 75, 77, 81, 137
North Sea 57, 127, 129, 135, 141
North York Moors (National Park) 25, 104, 107, 109, 113 – 115, 129, 136
North York Moors Railway 127, 133

O
Oddendale 70
Old Gang Mines 97

P
Patterdale 45, 51, 52, 54 – 56, 60, 141
Pennines 64, 69, 71 – 73, 78, 79, 99, 109, 138
Pennine Way 90, 91
Peter (Wainwright) 55
Place Fell 54
Pillar 34

R
Raven Seat 77, 78
Reeth 84, 87, 98
Richmond 87, 91, 98 – 101, 107, 109, 110, 113, 117, 120, 137
River Esk 133
River Liza 33
River Swale 80, 87, 92, 94, 99, 101, 109, 110, 120
Robin Hood's Bay 24 – 26, 33, 89, 127, 135, 137 – 139
Robin Hood's Chair 33
Roseberry Topping 118
Rosthwaite 38, 42, 45, 47, 48
Round Hill 119
Ruth (Wainwright) 55

S
Sellafield 29
Shap 42, 45, 47, 56, 59, 67, 69, 70
Shap Abbey 59
St Bees 20, 25, 89, 137, 138
St Bees Head 24, 26, 28, 139
Swaledale 67, 69, 72, 75, 78 – 80, 87, 89, 91, 92, 96, 98, 100, 101, 137
Swan Inn 113
Swinner Gill Beck 94

T
Tenzing Norgay 52

U
Ullswater 45, 50, 53, 54, 61

V
Vale of Mowbray 104, 107, 109, 112, 113, 117, 120, 137, 138

W
Wainstones 107, 118
Whitsundale 77
William Wordsworth 50

Y
Yorkshire 76, 79, 81, 112, 129
Yorkshire Dales (National Park) 25, 69, 76, 118